American Politics

Occam's Razor Series, Volume 2

JD Lovil

Published by JD Lovil Publishing, 2019.

While every precaution has been taken in the preparation of this book, the publisher assumes no responsibility for errors or omissions, or for damages resulting from the use of the information contained herein.

AMERICAN POLITICS

First edition. July 6, 2019.

ISBN: 978-1393329978

Written by JD Lovil.

Also by JD Lovil

Table of Contents

Disclaimer

THIS BOOK WILL ATTEMPT to discuss the characteristics of politics in America. The Author will attempt to introduce his opinion of the situation and circumstances in the universe of discourse, and use the argumentative tools, including Occam's Razor to critique the logical conclusions reached.

The subject matter of this book is open to extreme interpretations and viewpoints. The Author has taken the opportunity to add his discordant voice into the mix, with the hope of adding clarity to these muddy waters. If he cannot do that, he will settle for adding mud into these clear waters. Whatever works.

ACKNOWLEDGMENTS

THIS BOOK IS BASED primarily on my observations of the various elements of the political machine here in the United States over the course of my life. There is much to admire, and much to fear in our legacy of political apparatus.

The information and experiences that form the bulk of this book come from an enormous number of sources. The Author has a definite Libertarian bent, and a tendency to favor that viewpoint over any other viewpoint. Be warned.

The Author also is violently opposed to being politically correct, a conversational policy which he considers to be a form of social bullying. In consequence, be warned that he will not be using euphemisms such as gender-neutral language, hyphenated appellations, or avoiding phrases that past generations found good, but which the current social police consider bad. I will be calling the native tribes of this nation Indians, not Native-Americans. I will not be calling darker skinned persons Afro-Americans unless they once lived in Africa.

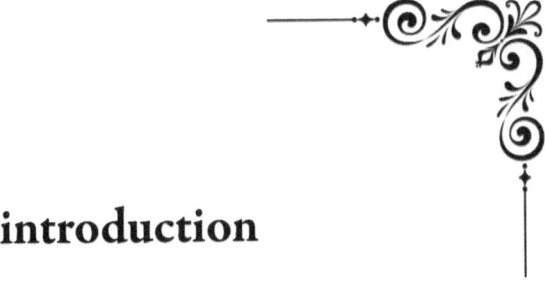

introduction

OCCAM'S RAZOR- a philosophical principle, applied to the field of scientific inquiry and to the resolution of logical arguments, which states that the simplest theory that explains all of the facts relating to the argument is probably the correct one.

They cannot all be right. There has to be a method to define the argument in such a way that it is possible to find the true answers in this ocean of wishful speculation that currently holds sway as the answers. It is time for a closer look at how to use the tool we call Occam's Razor to find the answers.

Occam's Razor is a principle that is more appropriate for scientific inquiry than it is for the normal argumentative procedure. Let me explain what I mean by that.

A scientific investigation has many of the elements of a logical argument. It assembles all of the known facts. It assembles the possible conditions and mechanisms that explain the facts. These are all speculated upon, and the hypotheses that are formed to explain the phenomena are advanced as tentative assumptions that are easily changed, eliminated, or abandoned. It eventually reaches a conclusion which explains the whole process under investigation in every case.

The conclusion is the theory that we make out of the argument. If we find even one case in which the theory does not accurately explain the events, we must abandon that theory for an alternative explanation.

We find it to be quite useful to filter through our possible answers in such a scientific inquiry using Occam's Razor. It works well as a tool to uncover the truth when the seeker has not already made up their mind about what is going on, but it might also be used to damage a logical argument where the participants have already decided what conclusions they wish to reach in the argument.

In either the scientific or the simple logical arguments, some components are essential to use in the argument's structure. Let us discuss the structure familiarly and informally.

As is true for any journey, an argument starts with some sort of roadmap. The two sides have to agree on the subject of the argument. In some forms of argument, they may also state their intended conclusions. In other forms, they will let the argument lead them to the conclusion.

They will assemble a set of assumptions that support their arguments. These will divide into two sets of assumptions. The first set will be the assumptions that both sides of the argument can agree are valid without revision. The second set will be the assumptions that are in dispute by one or both sides without revision, but that both sides may be persuaded to accept during the process of the argument.

The argument will need to supply facts and evidence to support any aspect of the argument that is not wholly accepted by the other side. In the case of the question of alien life and visitation, this might include testimonies of witnesses, photographic, and physical evidence, and various sorts of numerical analysis.

Rules will also be required to reach valid conclusions by logical means. One of the worst qualities of any form of argument is the tendency of one of the participants to 'drown out' their opponent, or overpower and intimidate them, to win by default.

Tune in any current political debate, and you will see one side continue to talk out of turn and above the opponent's comments, to silence them. If I were the drowned out participant, then I would have one of two reactions.

I might tend to be somewhat sad that my opponent had so little logical thought that intimidation techniques were the 'go to' methods for their arguments, and wonder why the moderator had not switched off my opponent's microphone when they began doing the 'talk over.' I might also have the urge to reach over and rearrange their faces with extreme prejudice if I had an even slightly bad day.

This process of drowning out one side of the match is damaging in that it nullifies the purpose of the logical argument, and it allows the logical conclusion to be a flawed conclusion since the basis of the argument depends on competition rather than logic. Logic is a deliberative process, not a competitive process.

Because logic is deliberative, the persons who are good at using it are usually also deliberative and analytical, only presenting their points as factual points after careful scrutiny. This makes the logical personality slow to speak, and easy to be 'yelled down' by a more competitive person.

This all leads to a principle I like to call **the ten-year-old girl principle**. A two-hundred-pound man usually has nothing to fear from a match-up with a sixty-five or seventy-pound ten-year-old girl. All he has to do is retaliate with minimal strength, or subdue her by sitting on her or putting her in an arm or headlock. He can even just walk away.

If someone restrained the man by rules that forced him not to walk away, and not to attack or defend himself overtly or covertly, then he would suddenly find himself in danger. It might take a while, but the ten-year-old would eventually be able to beat the man to death.

When a person is engaged in an argument in a deliberative methodology, while his opponent is acting competitively, the competitive methodology will win, even though it does not achieve the results that they should be seeking. In order to reach any sort of valid investigative conclusion, both sides of the argument should be using the deliberative methods. When deciding which of several possible conclusions might be the correct one, the use of Occam's Razor is very useful.

Arguments generally are used as tools in two different ways. One use of arguments is as a means to determine the truth in the subject they discuss. They may also be used to justify the conclusion that one or both of the participants wish to reach. I will give you two guesses about which way is the right way to use logic.

Logic is a way to lead the opponent to a conclusion about a subject, which is acceptable to both parties. This can be about actions to take, or this can be a process to understand. The conclusion can be a pre-determined conclusion that the first party wishes to convince the second party is the superior conclusion, or it can be a conclusion that is wholly determined by where the stairway of the acceptable assumptions leads.

While the steps of a logical argument must be logical, the conclusion may be irrational. For instance, consider the following idea:

I want a vehicle to drive to destinations in my life. It will be mostly in town on city streets, and I do not need a work truck, so a car will be acceptable. Four wheels, engine, and the normal accouterments are all necessary components.

I can let my logical ladder of assumptions and facts lead me to an arbitrary conclusion, and wind up with a Ford Fuckus, or some similar vehicle. Alternatively, I can start out with my secret desire for a red Corvette, and design my logical argument to reach the conclusion that the red Corvette is my perfect car. It all depends on what the purpose of the argument is as to which form my argument should take.

If I truly want to wind up with the perfect car for my needs, I probably will not be getting the red Corvette. If I need a proper ego stroking, then the Corvette is the only conclusion that will do.

If we call the two techniques of logical argument the investigative and the egocentric, then obviously the investigative is most useful for learning new things, and taking care to find the truth rather than your preferred lies. The egocentric is good for getting what you want, not for learning the truth. Both forms are used extensively in the subjects of current and preferred American Politics.

Once all of the assumptions and facts have been considered in the subject of all things political, Occam's Razor becomes absolutely necessary for determining which of the possible conclusions are the most likely ones to be the valid conclusions. In case you don't know how it goes, I will restate it below.

Occam's Razor- a philosophical principle, applied to the field of scientific inquiry and to the resolution of logical arguments, which states that the simplest theory that explains all of the facts relating to the argument is probably the correct one.

Some possible conclusions can be reached regarding the questions that we can raise about the best form of politics. Here are some below.

1. A good government increases individual freedom.

A Yes it does.

B No, it does not.

2. Do we have a democracy, or something else?

A. No.

B. Yes.

3. Is our government actually of the form it claims to be, or is it deceiving the American people?

A. Our government is really a good democracy.

B. Our government is really run by a bunch of power-hungry people that have no interest in our best interests.

The number of possible questions to answer in this area are endless, and then there are the sub-questions to answer. For instance, is our government currently in the form that it was supposed to be, and if so, is it working correctly?

We will be touching on the subjects that are most valid to determine the political ins and outs of the nature of current American politics. I must warn you that this subject covers a whole lot of ground.

Buckle your seatbelts, and crank up your model A. It is time to go talk to the Founding Fathers.

1 GOVERNMENT FORMS

WE WILL BEGIN OUR DISCUSSION on politics by defining a number of possible forms that the government can take. The average American knows little or nothing about most of them. Even the forms of Kingdoms have been simplified by our various forms of media to satisfy our need for history at the expense of our understanding. Let us start by discussing what a Kingdom is.

Kingdom: A country, state, or territory ruled by a king or queen.

There are a large number of variations of this form of government. At one time, virtually every village had a chieftain that considered himself a king. It wasn't long before the big fish ate up the little fish, leaving the weaker kings, or their replacements, to rule over the surrendered territory for the big king. Sooner or later, there was only one acknowledged 'High King' in most of these so-called nations, and he was acknowledged as the supreme authority by a bunch of lower kings.

Since it got a little confusing to call everyone you met king, the title of the lower kings soon was changed to that of Duke, or whatever the local equivalent turned out to be. Even the dukes needed some help with their territory, and so along came the titles of Count or Earl (Jarl in the Norse) to keep everyone working for the man.

Local politics and simple economics demanded that certain large parcels of land should be gifted to special people who were loyal to the

9

royal hierarchy, and who could be counted on to support the kingdom. These large landholders became the Barony.

If you translate these positions into modern American political terms, then this might be an understandable breakdown:

King (Monarch) would be the equivalent of our President.

Dukes would be the equivalent of our Governors.

Counts would be the equivalent of our County Governments in the form of one person.

Barons would be the influential landowners in each of these counties.

Unfortunately, this form of government has a habit of rapidly becoming one for the benefit of the rulers, with the welfare of the common man at the whim of the greedy. It is this form of ruler that the pilgrims and most of the rest of our American forefathers came to the New World to escape from.

The next form we should discuss is that of the Dictator, or sometimes they are called Autocrats. They usually rule under false pretenses. Much of the time, a bad regime is overthrown by a people's movement of some sort, only to install one of these guys in the role of supreme power.

Russia started down this road with its overthrow of the old royalty, only to use the pretext of Communist Socialism to gather power into the hands of the Socialist party, and then, over time, into the hands of a few rich and influential despots. It is an interesting situation when you can trust organized crime more than you can trust your own government, but that is what they have over there.

The Dictatorship can take many forms, or should we say disguises. The Castro family in Cuba told the world that they were simply the figureheads of a Socialist-Communist government, but in effect, they were simply dictators.

A Theocracy is a government that rules using the doctrines of one of the many parasitic religions of the world to authorize said rule. The most famous of the modern examples is the government of Iran.

The Priestly elite of the Shia Moslem sect rules Iran. They follow a version of Sharia Law that is definitely Old Testament eye for an eye stuff. It is interesting that however much the people suffer, the ruling elite keep getting richer.

Russia or China are both examples of what Socialism becomes when put to the test. Socialism is a form of government, which claims that the government will administer the resources of the country for the citizens.

It is a form of 'Daddy knows bestism.' The theory is that all money and resources will be dispensed to the citizenry according to their needs. By one method or another, all Industry is owned by the government, supposedly for the good of the people.

Socialism is supposed to progress to a form of Communism. Communism is the form where all Industry and resources are actually owned directly by the community instead of the State and dispensed according to need for each citizen.

In Russia, the badly formed Socialism did not really become Communism. Instead, the ruling elite became those party leaders who brutally ruled in the style of the Mafia, while the erstwhile citizen was reduced to a quasi-slave status.

In China, Socialism has become something almost bizarre. The State runs much of the Industry and is brutal about controlling the rest. Much of their GDP depends on pirating of intellectual properties and financial systems in a manner that would do the Vikings proud. Somehow, I think that they actually missed the whole idea of true communism.

Fascism is a form that is even harder to understand than is the Socialism-Communism system. Hitler's Third Reich was a Nationalist and Socialist form of Fascism, which had as a form of national pride the purity of a hypothetical Aryan race.

The problem with Fascism is that it mixes so well with other forms of government. For instance, it can be a Socialist form, or it can be one of the many forms of Dictatorships. I suppose that it could even be a form of Monarchy, as long as national identity is strongly tied up with whoever the king happens to be.

Now that science and business have caught up to politics, it could show up in the form of a Technocracy(government based on a technological advantage) or a Corporatocracy, which is a government run by corporations.

Regardless of what form a Fascist state takes, it is bad news for the bulk of its citizens, and ultimately, for all of them. It might well make the trains run on time, but with its disregard for the people that make it up, eventually, the only place the trains are going is to take the hapless millions is to an early grave.

One of the first examples of a Republic that we can describe is that of the Roman Empire. A Republic is a form of government, which has a ruler in the form of a Caesar or a president, with a group of representatives in the form of a Senate, which helps to some extent to enact laws and represent the interests of some category of the citizens.

In the case of the Roman Senate, while the Senators theoretically represented the Roman citizens, they were way too closely controlled by the Caesar to truly represent the people. This fault in the Empire was due to the dictatorial nature of the rulers of the empire.

When the Magna Carta was foisted on the English Crown at the point of a sword, it was one of the first examples of a constitution, and it precipitated in time the formation of a House of Lords, and a House of Commons. The two houses were supposed to respectively represent both the Royalty and the common citizens respectively, and, along with the Magna Carta, it was the first example of a Constitutional Republic that I am aware of, even though I don't believe they ever got around to calling it that.

One of the advantages of a Republican format is that only the representatives have to make the long trip to the Capital. Few people traveled more than fifty miles from the place of their birth until very recently, so asking the masses to represent themselves in a more democratic format was not practical.

Picking the best ideas from the British Tyranny, when our beleaguered ancestors decided to make a new nation, they decided to create a form of Democratic Republic that picked the best aspects of the English government to institute. They thought that a more democratic form of a Republic, backed up by a hard constitution was the ticket.

Before we discuss our particular take on democracy, we should briefly discuss the pure form of that format. We will start in the next paragraph.

The ancient Greeks get the credit for inventing democracy, although I would imagine that it probably had been invented hundreds of times before the Greeks existed. Generally speaking, democracy is an 'each citizen gets a vote' system. In the ancient world, its biggest drawback was that the democracy couldn't get very big, because the people couldn't go hiking across the country for every vote.

A second problem with democracy is that rule by consensus is usually pretty awkward compared to a single man making the decisions. This meant that the evil heathens could prance in and kill the democratic warriors before they got through voting. That is probably why the Greeks were famous for their sprinters. It is always handy to be able to outrun the man with the sword.

Now that we have struggled through all the more popular forms of government, it is time to describe what we have in our own good old United States of America. The next chapter will briefly talk about the historical hows, whys, and whats that went into the evolution of the American way.

We have what is technically a Constitutional Democratic Republic. The constitution is the core of our governmental format and laws and tells us what each person, state, or federal agency can or cannot do. We are democratic, because we vote on representatives and legal matters at the state levels, and vote for our federal representatives. We are a republic because we vote for the people that represent our interests in the federal legislative houses.

We will go into all of that in more depth in the following chapters.

2 AMEROPOLITICAL HISTORY

YOU PROBABLY THINK that you know American history, and for the general details, you are probably right. Every interpretation comes with a point of view, however, and the spin on historical details definitely **did not** miss American history.

You probably remember stuff like Columbus discovering America. You remember the landing of the Pilgrims, the Revolutionary War, and the Civil War. You remember some of all that other weird stuff that occurred within the last 150 years, but do you know what those things were **really** about? I will bet that most of the whys of what happened that you learned is wrong.

You know that Columbus discovered America while trying to find a good trade route to the East Asian world. You know that the American Colonies rebelled against the English King, and so began the Revolutionary War. This is all true as far as it goes, but as someone once said, let me tell you, "the rest of the story."

You think that the Civil war was the attempt by the North to free the slaves in the South, and you would be dead wrong. For the last 150 years, you think that all of the legislative and legal maneuverings that have gone on was the attempt to establish a bigger and better Federal government, and you would also be incorrect.

Let us skip the voyage of Columbus, and the landing of the Pilgrims, and start at the time shortly preceding the Revolutionary War. There is a lot about the activities of that time that most Americans never learned in school.

When the countryside began to open up to agriculture and a wide variety of infrastructure creation, there was a huge demand for laborers to do the work. Since these methods of filling jobs were legal at the time, we all know that slaves sometimes were purchased to do those jobs.

What is not so popularly known is that the vast majority of European immigrants that arrived on our shores were essentially penniless, and they commonly booked passage to the New World using a form of indenture contract.

Unlike the slaves, the indentured were not property, but their contracts were property. The contract holders could sell the contracts, or they could order the indentured to do whatever task they wanted them to complete.

In some parts of the new world, there were a few laws to protect the indentured servants from mistreatment. These laws were frequently ignored, and indentured servants nearing the end of their terms were frequently starved, beat to death, or killed outright. After all, the end of the contract meant that they were of no more use, and so there was no reason to keep them healthy anymore.

It was said that the indentured, who frequently worked side by side with the black slaves in the fields, frequently envied the slaves, who were treated much better than themselves, and kept in a much healthier state. Indenture started to go out of vogue before 1820, but until then, over half of the white immigrants arriving in America worked under these contracts.

Slavery became a popular source of labor due to their availability. The black Moslem Moors were raiders who made a living raiding various nearby regions, such as Spain (before they became too powerful) in Viking fashion. They also frequently abducted villagers from the various African tribes to sell as slaves to the highest bidders. That is how the slaves arrived in the New World.

Just before the civil war, the United States was a federation of states, with the South predominately agricultural, while the North engaged more in trade and manufacturing. The population in the South was mostly spread out over the countryside, while in the North, the population was concentrated in the cities.

Like a parody of the current times, concentrated city populations believed that they should be in charge of how things were run since the majority of the population lived there. The Southern states believed that they should be left alone to run their own states their own way, as the constitution allowed.

This is the first major breaking of the constitutional laws. War was declared when the South decided to take advantage of their constitutional right to secede from the Union, which was a prime right given by the Articles of Federation. Although the Articles of Federation had been replaced by the constitution, its content was an implicit feature of the new constitution.

Almost as an afterthought, the North enacted laws that made slavery illegal, thinking that this provided a good reason to impose their will on the South, and abolishing slavery would make the South weaker, and more compliant. What they did not realize was that slavery was already on its way out in the South, with such improvements as the cotton gin making the need for slave labor unnecessary.

I think that we all know how that war came out. Nobody that was not born in the South understands the true significance of its impact on the country, but everyone knows how it affected our country.

In typical aggravated human fashion, our country has been on a self-development bender ever since. If you went to school, you should be conversant with most of the big moves in our history since the Civil War, although most of the history written was written with a strong spin on it. We will selectively discuss these tidbits of history as they arise in future chapters.

3 FORMATION

IN THE TIME PERIOD from 1750 to 1776, things were getting worse with regard to relations with the British Empire, and the British Crown. Slightly more than half of the residents of the British colonies were getting the idea that their lives would be improved if the American colonies did not have to answer to the King.

At the start, all thirteen of the American colonies thought of themselves as independent from the others. When the idea of succession from the British Empire congealed, each of these colonies began to think of themselves as independent nations. They all realized that they would need some allies in any possible war, so some coordination was called for.

The King became increasingly harsh with the colonies as time wore on, and even the British loyalists reluctantly concluded that independence was necessary. There was a group of people that the modern world would call Influencers, and they proceeded to set to work to establish the framework.

If Facebook had existed in the mid-1700s, Ben Franklin would have been its inventor. Like most of the other Founding Fathers, he was a Free Mason and dabbled in other more esoteric societies. Collectively, the Founding Fathers were interested in creating a successful and long-lived collaboration between the colonies, with as little meddling in the rights and affairs of the citizens by the government as they could manage.

They envisioned a form of government that took only the best parts of British and other world governments and was carefully crafted around a constitution created to be an upgrade to the Magna Carta and all of the various forms of a constitution drafted to that time. Unfortunately, the colonies were not interested in becoming part of a country that had any power to tell them what to do. They considered themselves to be countries in their own right.

Because the colonies were so resistant to having a central federal government, the first article drawn up to unify the colonies to the extent that they would permit was the Articles of the Confederation. This document basically gave the overall government the right to raise an army, participate in negotiating trade agreements, alliances, and truces, and instituted a voluntary tax for the purpose of funding these actions.

Since the AOC specified the independence of the colonies, the colonies were happy to support that part of the document. As far as the standing army, depending on the new government to negotiate, and the taxation, these were taken under advisement.

The world revolved this way for a very few years until things got so bad that some ruffians in Boston decided to throw some tea overboard in Boston Harbor to protest British taxation. The King loved his tea and decided that it was time to punish the Massachusetts colony for daring to waste good Earl Grey.

The next three years was a time period in upheaval, as Britain prepared first to spank Massachusetts, then the rest of the colonies. The Brits sent in their Hessian contractors to try to put down uprisings all over the place after the official Declaration of Independence, and the war lasted from 1775 until 1783.

England had a very long supply line and was at a strategical disadvantage due to distance, but it was hard to imagine that the ill-trained commoners in America could defeat the armies of the Empire upon which the sun never set. Nonetheless, they did. Imagine what they could have done to the British if they had been unified in purpose, rather than scattering their efforts.

You know the general story. You have a mental image of General Washington, in his row-boat in the middle of the Potomac River. You know about the long line of Daniel Boone lookalikes that filled them Britty britches with buckshot on their way back across the pond. Well, musket balls, anyway.

The short story is that we won, and we got to make our own little world. There were Indians to mistreat, possums and raccoons to eat, and buffalo and other wildlife to eradicate. Shortly after, there were railroads to build, and further American shenanigans to participate in all over the world.

It wasn't until 1787 that everything settled down to the point where the Founding Fathers, who mostly survived the war in the proud tradition of partying in a safe place, to get down to the actual formation of the new Federal government, which has finally grown into the adult drug, sex, and power-crazed adult government that we all enjoy today.

Their efforts to make a good government that can rule those somewhat feral children of Liberty is the subject of the next chapter.

4 THE 3 BRANCHES

OUR GOOD OLE FOUNDING Fathers started stitching together what they considered the ideal form of government just as soon as they could get anybody to listen. They borrowed a lot of bits from the English system, added some other ideas from different parts of the world, and then they did a brainstorming session to make it work.

The main problem they wanted to prevent was the concentration of power in the hands of a few or even a single person. That is where the three branches and the constitution came into the picture.

The Constitution of the United States was created to state which powers belonged to which part of the government, the states, and the citizens. It also established the Executive, Legislative, and the Judicial branches to oversee specific parts of the federal government's activities.

The Federal government was never intended to be a superior force to the force of the individual states. Each state was looked at as an independent nation, but subject to the same constitution, and obligated to certain actions for the welfare of the states as a whole.

The Executive branch was the branch that was supposed to execute the laws of the land, as laid out by the Legislature, and interpreted by the Judicial branch. It was also supposed to be responsible for the operation of a military force to respond to threats against any or all of the states.

The formation of the CIA, the FBI, and all of the other alphabet agencies are the result of the cancerous growth of the executive branch power to execute the laws and to extend the executive power into a world that the Founding Fathers never foresaw. Our military force is also the modern mutation of a ready army of colonial times into whatever Orwellian world we now live in.

The Legislative branch was to be composed of two houses of representatives. The first one was patterned after the House of Commons of the English system. This was the Congress of Representatives, commonly called the Congress. It was supposed to be filled with popularly voted in farmers, doctors, janitors, or other common citizens, who would basically vote for what they wanted. Because they were not necessarily critical thinkers, they would then pass the bills they desired on to a second house to mold into legal form and discuss the relative merits of the idea.

The second house was patterned after the House of Lords and has always been filled with representatives that tended to be lawyers or other legal eagles. They were the Senate, and you could consider them to be the representatives of the states, just as the house of representatives could be considered the representatives of the citizens direct.

Once the bills or laws are passed by the Congress, it is sent to the President to be signed. If he signs it, it becomes law. Otherwise, he vetos it, and they either have to pass it through the Congress with a super-majority, or it will not become law.

Once a law becomes a law, if someone finds it to be unfair or hurtful, they can try to get a ruling on the bill by a judge on its validity. It quickly escalates all the way up to the Supreme Court, who can decide on the legitimacy of the law.

The Supreme Court is the highest representative agency of the Judicial branch. It has a single job on its agenda. It must examine any law brought to it, and decide whether or not the law conforms to that set of legal actions allowed by the constitution. If it does not, then it is bound to strike that law down as unconstitutional.

That is the basic structure of the government as formed by the Founding Fathers. The problem with governments is the same problem as for all organisms and all systems.

The problem is that systems grow. Like any living thing, it either grows, or it dies. Our government has grown and expanded its powers into thousands of places that it was never intended to have power over.

It is a sad tale. Fortunately, after decades of devoted effort, the powers that be have managed to dumb down the American population to the point that they no longer realize how far off the tracks this train of American politics has gotten.

We will discuss all of the various ways that it has grown into the behemoth that it is in the next few chapters.

5 THE CONSTITUTION

THE FOUNDATION OF THE newly created American republic was the constitution. It was intended to be the supreme law of the land. The Founding Fathers knew that the vote in the hands of an uninformed public was a dangerous weapon, and so the Constitution was intended to protect the people against their own shortsightedness.

Human nature is decidedly selfish. The old guys knew that. If you give someone the vote, you can be sure that most of the voters will not be thoughtful in their choices. Given ignorance, most voters will vote for the things they want, without considering the costs and consequences.

Voters will vote for bread and circuses, just as soon as they find out that they can vote for anything. If the majority of voters decide that the murder of some minority is good for them, they will vote for murder. The only protection against such bad voting is a constitution that is above all other laws of the country, even those enacted by representatives voted in by voters.

Let us consider a prime example. On a federal level, the Constitution protects the citizenry regarding the right to keep and bear arms. When a few people have been killed using firearms, the citizens of the area usually will decide that the firearms themselves are responsible, and they will vote to outlaw the possession of firearms.

The Constitution is the safeguard against the mutation of this republic into some form of tyranny. Only as long as the laws of the land conform to the conditions imposed by the Constitution are we assured of having true freedom and liberty.

Everyone has had the dismaying experience of being talked into something you don't want and don't need for a ridiculous price by a sleek tongued salesman. Voters are like that. Lawyers can talk you into anything, and make it sound like it is your own good idea. Most politicians have lawyer blood in them somewhere.

The Constitution provides for certain natural and unalienable rights of the citizenry. Maybe we should go through a few of these now. Let us try the one that is delineated in the amendments.

The Constitution specifies that every human has certain 'inalienable' rights. That means that they cannot be taken away from the person. Among these is the right to the pursuit of liberty and freedom. The general gist of the document is that every person should be free to do anything that does not hurt their fellow humans.

Selling food to a starving man for ungodly prices, such as trading his firstborn for a bowl of soup is considered to not be a freedom we enjoy. Selling a hungry man food for a vaguely reasonable price is our freedom. See the difference?

We have the freedom of speech according to the first amendment. This means that we can say anything that we want to say. This does not mean that someone might not answer us with a fist if they find it offensive.

We have the right to speak freely, and the right to profess our religious beliefs or acknowledge the same, and we have the right to not be forced to practice religious activities that we do not accept. Because we must be well informed in order to choose our actions wisely, we have the right to a free press to deliver news and information to us.

We have the right to bear arms. This is a primary right to prevent the encroachment of tyranny into our lives. Even though this amendment was created with the admonishment that 'it shall not be infringed,' there have been several infringements to this freedom over the years.

We have the right to be free from unreasonable searches and seizures. The government and its representatives have no right to invade our privacy or sanctity against our protests, and it has no right to seize our possessions without due process.

Many places in the world are prone to throwing innocent people into jail cells, beating and forcing a confession from them, and then punishing them for a crime that they did not commit. The Fifth Amendment gives persons accused of crimes the right not to incriminate themselves, and to prevent them from being tried for the same crime twice. It is sort of against the coercion of confessions in addition to the legal boilerplate.

In combination with the Fourteenth Amendment, it also ensures our right to 'due process' before they can sentence you. Another way to say that is 'give you a fair trial before they hang you.'

The Constitution also states that you have the right to just compensation (a fair price) before the government can take something you own. If you do not want to lose your farm, this doesn't help, but if you would sell it for the right price, this (theoretically) guarantees that you get that fair price.

You are guaranteed the right to a fair and speedy public trial, the right to legal counsel, and that you will not be punished in a cruel and unusual way. Killing you by dismemberment, or forcing you to drink Clorox until dead are strictly illegal.

There are a lot more subjects covered in the Constitution and its amendments, such as the abolishment of slavery, equal protection, women's rights to vote, and a lot of boring language necessary to ensure the proper function of a government, but you probably get the idea by now. If you want to explore the Constitution, its amendments, or the Bill of Rights in more depth, the answers are no further away than Google.

6 DEGENERATION

WE HAVE THE BIGGEST, most expensive and most dysfunctional government that the world has ever seen. There are a lot of good things about living in America, but there are also a lot of definite drawbacks.

If our government was operating effectively, we could state that we live in a Constitutional Democratic Republic, but due to a lot of lazy representatives, it has turned into a big Bureaucracy. It has been a long time since Congress has done its job properly, usually delegating its responsibilities to the President and the various agencies of the Executive branch. They then complain when the President exercises the powers that the Congress ceded to him.

The biggest defense that the Founding Fathers put into place to make certain that the high population states could not tyrannize the lower population states was the Electoral College. They foresaw a time when the collective populations of the cities could vote for the things they wanted, even if that vote would hurt the farmers and other rural industries. I think that someone forgot to explain that little detail in modern schools.

Don't get me wrong. There are some problems with the way our Republic and its built-in protections are constructed. Maybe we need to start from general assumptions that were mistaken, and then go into the various conditions that the Founding Father never imagined might one day exist.

One of the issues that confront most of us at one time or another is laws and regulations that force us to act in a manner that is against our natures. These usually fall into specific categories of activity.

You will find these discrepancies in lawful actions in areas of activity such as sexual activities, defensive aggression, and environments that have an adverse effect on your social standing. A prime example of this is in self-defense situations, where the culprit is destroying your property, acting in a menacing manner, or making you feel challenged and insulted without actually forcing you to defend the life of yourself or your loved ones.

The fact is that men have an inbuilt need to defend their possessions and their relationships against intruders. Our instincts call for the elimination of the intruders, which means that there will always be men that are killed in a cheating wife's bed and self-defense cases that are ruined by the intruders being shot in the back as they are leaving.

As long as laws are made which do not uphold our natural instincts for dealing with the situations, there will be a certain percentage of the imprisoned that are truly guilty of nothing except being unable to stifle their natural instincts. We all lie to ourselves about our true natures. These lies find themselves embedded in our legal system, and some poor jerk will always pay the price for that lie.

The Founding Fathers could never have conceived of the progress that has been made in the art of war. In their day, if a man had a musket, he was equivalently armed to any soldier of the times.

With those simple armaments in mind, the Founding Fathers worried that any government could become a tyranny, and they knew that the only solution for this tendency was a revolution. It was with this in mind that the Second Amendment was written.

The Second Amendment states, "The right of the citizenry to keep and bear arms shall not be infringed." If that needs interpretation, they were saying that nothing was lawful that kept any citizen from possessing any armament they wished to own.

In today's world, according to the Second Amendment, you are allowed, maybe even encouraged, to own your very own nuclear bomb. If you have room in your back yard, you can set up a ballistic missile back there to carry the bomb off to destroy your enemies. It was thought that said missile would be used to stop a tyrannical American government from telling you what to do.

Today we have a bunch of idiots trying to tell us what is best for us. Most of the 'new' ideas from the Democrats in charge are nothing more than recycled socialism. The particular socialism programs they would like to institute would do absolutely nothing good, and even the smallest of them would bankrupt the country to institute.

The regular Republicans are no better. The solution to every problem for them is either to start another war or to take over the 'enemy' by using our endless stream of currency to buy their compliance to the American way.

As I stated before, I am in the Libertarian camp. Most Americans are libertarians, but most of those do not know that they are libertarians. The only parties in this country that have a shot at winning an election is the Democrats and the Republicans. We are stuck with the crazy people.

In short, we are in a sorry state, on the lip of catastrophe, or even possibly over the edge of the chasm. If it is not already too late, we need to correct our course immediately, or we will surely lose this wonderful country that we are blessed to live in.

In the next chapter, I will have a short rant about how our history has been rewritten by persons with ulterior motives, and what really happened. The clearest changed history is about the Civil War, so I hope that you will bear with me, regardless of your political preferences.

OCCAM'S RAZOR

I THINK THAT IT IS obvious that the government is not working properly. Can we think of a good way to fix things, so they work correctly? I don't believe there would be any real problem making things a lot better than they are right now.

The first thing I can imagine doing that would help make the government work correctly is to fix the incessant fighting between the various branches so that they are actually doing those things they are empowered to do, and leaving those things they are not empowered to the branches that are empowered to do them.

For instance, Congress has always been empowered to declare war by the simple act of financing it, using legislation to create legitimate funding. The president has always been supposed to be the basic commander-in-chief, creating a general policy regarding how wars are fought and acting to fill in command function in emergencies that do not allow time for the Congress to act.

Currently, Congress hasn't been very much involved in the act of declaring war. Instead, they have ceded their responsibilities, allowing the president's in recent decades to declare war on their own.

Because Congress has ceded their responsibilities, recent presidents have not been prone to ask them for their permission to declare war. This needs to stop. Our country has been involved in many wars recently that we really had no right or need to be in.

Part of the reasons why the presidents have been so volatile in declaring war is because their subordinates tend to be war hawks. The way a typical bureaucrat gets power is by doing things that are notorious. I will give you an example.

John Bolton is currently an advisor to the president in situations that call for a war footing in his opinion. Unfortunately, he thinks a war footing is required in almost every case. While I consider John to be well-meaning, he seems to have only that one note in his To-Do list.

There are three branches of our government. There is a legislative branch consisting of the House of Representatives and the Senate, the executive branch consisting of the president and the necessary agencies for his function, and the judicial branch consisting of the lower courts and the Supreme Court.

The House of Representatives is supposed to create new legislation according to the citizens' wishes and desires. The Senate is supposed to give the House of Representatives feedback, refine the legislation and then to either vote it down or vote for it.

You can think of the House of Representatives as being a bunch of pretty faces that the citizens voted into office because they like the way they looked and acted and they thought they'd give them what they wanted. Unfortunately, the House of Representatives is actually are just a bunch of pretty faces, with empty heads and absolutely no scruples.

You can think of the Senate as a bunch of slimy lawyers. They are supposed to debate endlessly about the merits of a particular new piece of legislation, and then modify that legislation so that it actually can become law. It is probably wise it was set up that way because the House of Representatives is pretty terrible about creating new laws that do not make sense.

The problems with these two sections of that legislative branch are that they're not very functional. Too many of them become lifelong politicians looking for power. Most of them are beholden to rich benefactors; either donors or companies, and they forget about doing the will of the people.

Occam's razor would say that they are some simple solutions that would make things work much better. They should be forced to have term limits, and they should also not be allowed to leave town without doing their duty in terms of passing laws. That is one power that the government should give to the president, which is to force the legislators to stay in session until they are done with a specific piece of legislation.

The legislative branch has the basic duties to create new laws and to fund the actions of the government. They were never supposed to act as a court and to themselves like they are doing right now with the Never-Trump fervor that is happening at this moment.

One of the more important functions of the legislative branch, specifically the House of Representatives, is to oversee the other branches, to make sure they don't overreach their own allotted powers. Currently, the legislative branch really doesn't do this very well. Instead, they are using it as a sort of political circus, where they tend only to grandstand for the microphones.

Occam's razor would suggest that the proper fix for this and other problems with the legislative branch would be a limitation on tenure for the branch representatives. A state by state no-confidence vote periodically given to remove the bad actors from the legislative branch when they don't conform to the will of the people would be advisable. Oversight of those two sides of that branch by the other branches would be essential.

The executive branch consists primarily of the president and those agencies which supports his activities. The president is supposed to sign or veto new legislation. He is supposed to act as commander-in-chief for the federal military and federal police agencies, although the existence of federal police agencies is a relatively new development and not entirely covered by the constitutional power conventions.

Occam's razor would suggest that a strong and harsh pruning of the executive branch is called for. The elimination of the educational and social programs, along with HUD, would be prudent. Those functions should be remanded to the state level. The IRS should be severely curtailed as a subordinate function of the treasury department, and the IRS court system should be eliminated and those functions remanded to the common judicial system.

The judicial branch consists of the courts of the land culminating in the Supreme Court. When a person or group seeks redress against an unfair law or an act by another person or group, they can use the court system to find a solution for their grievances.

The courts are always supposed to consider the constitutionality of any action they take and use the constitutionality of any action taken by other parties as a criterion for their judgments. If the parties involved decide that they cannot accept the judgment of the lower court, they can pass that judgment on to appellate courts and then eventually to the Supreme Court.

The Supreme Court is supposed to consider all cases before it through the lens of constitutionality only. It should not make a difference to them what the political viewpoint is of any party involved on any topic, it should only make a difference rather or not it is in accordance with the Constitution.

Needless to say, our current court system is almost exclusively made up of politically leaning judges. Instead of ignoring their personal bias, it has become necessary of late to balance the bias on the bench to allow for reasonably credible judgments.

Occam's razor would suggest to us that a more suitable set of criteria than acceptance by a political party would be advisable for constituting the makeup of the court system. Perhaps if we had a minimal test of adherence to constitutionality before the selection process took place, we would receive better results in regard to the court's composition.

As one might expect for any system or machine, over time, the gears of government become worn and need to be repaired. Most of the problems that we are experiencing now are the result of improper oversight or overreach of power on the parts of one or more of the branches of government.

It becomes customary for our country to think that bigger is better and that every solution has to be part of a package deal. An example of this, of course, has been the immigration laws of the country. We do indeed need to modify our immigration laws, and in some cases simply enforce them, but pushing any big package through is almost impossible.

Occam's razor says that the solution is to analyze each problem, come up with steps on the path to solving that problem, and then institute each step in sequence until you achieve the results that you want. In the case of immigration, we do not need to create a bill that solves all of our immigration problems at once. If we create a bill with solves the border security issues, and one that solves the dispensation of illegals currently living in this country, and one which resolves problems with how people legally become residents of this country, then we will have achieved everything we really need to do to fix the immigration problems.

7 CHANGED HISTORY

BEFORE WE GO ANY FURTHER into the somewhat muddy swamp of modern American politics, we need to recap a few historical details that are generally mangled by our current educational system. We will start with the various sorts of slavery that helped us establish and expand our country and proceed into the causes and consequences of the Civil War.

When the country was barely begun, the land available to be possessed by our greedy forebears seemed infinite. The number of affluent Landowners was insufficient to take advantage of this, and they had no desire to do all of the work for themselves.

Fortunately for them, they had two sources of almost endless labor that they could cheaply tap. The best known of these were slaves sold by Moslem pirates, taken from many of the different tribal villages of Africa.

The black slaves of Africa were owned by the people who bought them. This made them prized and valuable possessions. The second form of labor was indentured servants. While they were not owned by other people, there were contracts that required them to labor for the contract owners for a specific number of years.

The slaves were well-treated because the owner didn't want to damage their property, any more than you would want to damage your shiny new car. The indentured servants were treated horribly because the owners wanted to wrest every last drop of labor out of them that they could before the contract ran out.

This meant that the slaves were frequently forgiven their mistakes or behavior, while the servants were beaten and mistreated for their smallest transgressions. It was said that the indentured servants frequently envied the slaves when they toiled side by side in the fields.

Even today, in the South, you will find large farm properties with white owners surrounded by smaller farms owned by black families with the same last name as the white farm owners. This is because the black slaves became to be regarded as part of the family, and they were frequently given their own farmland as a token of the owner's esteem.

You do not find that same distribution of lands given to the indentured servants. Usually, if they survived the indenture period, they found themselves homeless and in distress unless they were very lucky. Many of them found themselves trying to make a new life out on the frontiers of the new country. That is where a large number of the cowboys and miners of our history came from.

The influx of indentured servants came about because there were many people from Europe who found the need to migrate to the New World, but they did not have the money for passage. They would sell their indenture to the ship captains, who would resell the contract to landowners in America.

Indentured servants were a dominating percentage of the new immigrants to the New World during a period before the Revolutionary War to about the 1820s. There was a slow-down in new contracts for about 20 years, until the time of the Irish Potato Famine forced a large segment of Northern European immigrants to again take up contracts to get to America.

By the decade of the Civil War, both slavery and indentured servitude were on their way out. The idea of share-cropping was making both ideas obsolete.

Up until the Civil War, the individual states considered themselves and treated each other as though they were independent countries. When they traded with each other, they would make deals and trade agreements to protect their interests.

The Northern states concentrated on industry, manufacturing, and trade, while the South produced tobacco, cotton, and whiskey as their primary exports. Both regions produced their own food supplies.

This arrangement worked pretty well, with about 60 percent of the population residing in the north, and about 40 percent living in the south. The North got uppity about control over the country and decided to turn the South into its own version of slavery.

They decided that they could force the South into an inferior position with the use of tariffs, levying higher and higher taxes on the goods imported from the South. They figured that they could be the controlling partner in this trading process.

The South didn't like that and decided to withdraw from the Union. The common interpretation of the Constitution gave them to right to secede, and so they decided to avail themselves of that right.

In short order, the North decided that they needed to stop the separation, and so the Civil War began. Thousands of white and black Southerners signed up to fight against the Union transgressors, and we all know the tales of the bloody war that followed.

It was not until the last half of the war that Lincoln reluctantly gave his famous speech against slavery, and linked it back to the war as a plausible reason to justify the Civil War. The North had no problem with slavery. Many of the Northern states still allowed the owning of slaves, and many Northerners still used them.

You know the story from here. The South lost the war. The North continued to suppress the South, forcing many changes to the southern way of life, importing sleazy politicians to change whatever they wanted to change about the South from the inside, so to speak.

The Civil War was the first time that both the spirit and the laws of the Constitution were broken in a significant way. Ever since that time, the political elite has made a habit of degrading or ignoring the constitutional requirements any time they wished to do so.

There are many areas of life, such as education, rights to armament, travel and other important 'rights given by God' that have become areas controlled by the government, rather than by the states or the citizens as specified in the Constitution. Our Federal government is like that snoopy next-door neighbor that happens to also be a cop that cannot resist micromanaging our lives while leaving their own lives a mess.

At any rate, now we spend endless blood and resources acting as the police for the rest of the world. They try to make sure that there is a federal law covering every act that we could possibly commit. They act to limit the access we have to arm ourselves as law-abiding citizens while doing nothing (possibly even promoting) the activity of criminals that have no interest in obeying these or any other laws.

Our country is a mess. While I do love this place, our country is like a dysfunctional family with a crack-head daughter, a heroin-addicted son, a mother with a wandering eye, and an alcoholic father. We probably need to organize our own affairs before we try to reorganize everyone else's house.

Now that we have put the introductory stuff behind us, we can start looking at all the categories of actions on the part of the political world and start deciding what is being done wrong, or even right in some rare cases. Once we find the problems, maybe we can find some useful fixes for those problems.

OCCAM'S RAZOR

IT IS OBVIOUS FROM the strange misinterpretations and misunderstandings of our history that someone somewhere does not want us to know our true history. In other words, someone is trying to condition a certain alteration of history understanding for the common American citizen.

People are so intent on making our history politically correct that they no longer have any true understanding of what actually took place. We're going through a period in which the statues and other historical relics are being torn down as some sort of angry reaction to imperfect historical figures.

The fact is that our peoples all are immigrants. No one, including the American Indians, is natives to this land. It is certainly true that according to modern sensibilities, there have been many grave injustices done to many groups of peoples. Among these groups, one can include the native American Indians. Overall, these injustices have been less than those in most other countries, and they are understandable given the circumstances under which they occurred.

When we suggest that the American Indians are deserving of restitution for taking their land and the other things that happen to them, it is important that we keep in mind that their belief in land ownership did not match our belief in land ownership at all, and they had a tendency to take land from other tribes throughout their history. When we consider slavery, we should also keep in mind that most of the white settlers in this country originally started out as indentured servants, which was actually a much more egregious form of slavery than ever occurred to the Blacks.

Occam's razor would suggest that we need to stop advancing actions along politically correct lines and start thinking about actual and meaningful improvements that we can make to our reactions to groups that actually work for this current time. We do not have any particular guilt that we should be carrying around about what happened between previous generations. They were not us, and we are not guilty of whatever it is we think was done wrong.

We have a lot to account for in our lives. We have a lot to do to make our lives better and to make things work for us, and it's time for us to get on with the business of improving our lives while we still have the means to do so.

Enough said about this particular subject. It deserves no more attention than we've paid it so far, and now we will turn our attention to other aspects of our government that needs to be repaired.

8 SIZE MATTERS

THE FOUNDING FATHERS created the components of the Federal government to limit its power to only the necessary power. They expected it to be small, and any power not allotted to it by the Constitutional framework would be the province of the states, or the citizens within those states, depending on which level of government would be most effective.

They created the three branches of the government to see to the manifest needs of the Federation of States. They intended the primary actions of the Federal government to be the coordination of forces in the event of war in the case of the executive branch. They thought that the Legislative branch would deal with the legal issues that came up between the states, and would act to vote on the funding of the few actions needed to be undertaken by the Federal government.

They intended the judicial branch to act to preserve the adhesion to constitutional principles and to adjudicate the legality of actions taken by federal and state actions, and act as a wall against the Legislative branch or the Executive branches taking unconstitutional actions.

They expected the journalistic section of the world to act as informational dispensers to bring light to improper actions on any of these avenues. The one thing they were certain of was that big government always led to the loss of freedoms. They knew that that would be the end of the American dream.

Every organism either grows, or it dies. The more cynical of the Founding Fathers knew that governments were just another form of an organism, and when the government grew too large, everything it did would become about growing larger. When the government's activity became all about growing, one by one, all of the freedoms of the American citizenry would begin to fall, and the country would inevitably become a tyranny.

We are at the point most feared at this point in time. One by one, the Federal government has begun eroding the liberty of the American people to do what they want to do. Soon, if it is not already too late, we will have no natural or constitutional freedoms at all. Soon, the government will be by and for the government, not for the people.

In case you are wondering, both major parties are big-government parties. The Republicans want a big government so that we can impose our will on the rest of the world. The Democrats want a big government because it has to be big to conduct all of the social programs they want to create. Also, it will use those programs to impose the Democrat's will on the people of the United States.

In the last two years, the Democratic Party has actually become the Democratic Socialist party. If the Democrats needed a big government, the socialists would need a super-sized government.

Unless we make a conscious and painful effort to reduce the size of our federal government, our freedoms *will* be taken away from us. It is a cast-iron guarantee if we do not reduce the size soon.

OCCAM'S RAZOR

THE FOUNDING FATHERS never envisioned a government nearly as large as the one we have. The small government that they envisioned had limited functions, and could easily find ways to constitutionally fulfill their duties. Not so with the government of today.

Today we have a government that attempts to do everything possible for everyone. Most of what it attempts to do are constitutionally illegal because the powers of the government at the federal level are supposed to be extremely limited.

There was no provision in the Constitution for the federal government to fulfill a function of educational, housing, or other similar roles. The social programs that the government attempts to fulfill at this time were considered at that time to be a family matter best handled by the family.

Since the government of the time had no standing army, and the citizens of the country would rise up with their personal arms at the need to defend the country, the Constitution makes no true distinction between an armed army and an armed citizenry. This means that according to the Constitution, if rocket launchers, nuclear weapons, and other high tech weapons exist, they cannot constitutionally be denied to the private citizens.

Obviously, that doesn't work so well in the real world that we find ourselves in today, but if we shed the Constitution, we will find ourselves in a nondemocratic and tyrannical despotic government shortly. We must find a way to allow the Constitution to exist alongside the realities of modern life.

Occam's razor suggests that we will probably find ourselves at some point soon in a position where we will have to do a certain amount of revision of the Constitution in order to continue to follow it. We must be very careful not to destroy the spirit of the Constitution in the act of attempting to modify the wording to allow full use of the document.

Certainly, a lot of things that are currently unconstitutional are also not necessary. There are no real valid reasons why the IRS, HUD, education agencies, and many other such agencies should exist when all of these agencies are taking actions which are in the provinces of the various states.

Once we have pruned down the size of the government to a level that is constitutional, we will also find that it is far more manageable and efficient. There are many things which the federal government concerns itself with that are no business of the feds.

Among these are such things as abortion, armament, licensing of such things as driver and business licensing, and of course the extensive meddling in our privacy which was afforded to the government by that evil document known as the Patriot Act. All of these things are either the Providence of the states, a local matter, or totally illegal in the first place.

We can go on and on about the many things that the government is doing that are illegal or ill-advised or in some way unconstitutional. Suffice it to say that removing 95% of the regulations, and making every new piece of legislation pass a "constitutional smell test" would be most prudent and most efficient.

We will doubtlessly get into a number of these topics in later chapters, but for now, let us just leave it at "we need to get rid of a whole lot of government."

9 GUNS

IF THERE IS A FUNDAMENTAL issue that demonstrates the difference between the Liberal and the Conservative factions of the population, it is the ownership and regulation of firearms. The second amendment is the fatal wall protecting the Constitution, and if it is abrogated, then the time of the Constitutional Republic is over.

"A well regulated Militia, being necessary to the security of a free State, the right of the people to keep and bear Arms shall not be infringed."

Let us break the Second Amendment down a little so that we can see precisely what it is saying. In the time this was ratified, the country did not possess a standing army. Instead, when the need for war arrived, each citizen of fighting age would grab their muskets, and go to defend their country.

The amendment served two primary purposes. First was the need for there to be armed citizens to call on in time of war. The second purpose was that everyone feared the government becoming tyrannical in the future, and then the citizenry would need to be able to forcefully stop it from turning everyone into slaves.

The 2nd Amendment gives everyone the right to own and carry their weapons. It is not saying the right to keep and bear arms is to be contained within some imposed limits. It does not say that you can own a weapon, but that the government can put conditions on your possession of that weapon.

The key phrase in the Second Amendment is "the right of the people to keep and bear Arms *shall not be infringed*." Notice that it says nothing about the type of weapon, or what it is used for, or that *anyone* has the right to restrict those weapons.

According to this phrase, nobody has the right to restrict *anyone's* possession of *any* weapon, no matter what it is. At the time the amendment was created, this wasn't a problem since nobody had created nuclear weapons, missile technology, or any of the other weapons of mass destruction that exist today.

While it is obvious that allowing anyone who wanted one to own their own nuclear bomb is a bad idea, there has been no modification of the amendment to restrict such ownership. Until such modification is created, restricting the right to own nuclear weapons, so-called assault weapons, or any other weapon is strictly unconstitutional.

The Second Amendment is not about hunting, or civilian self-defense, although it does not say that those are not legal uses of the weapons. It is about defending the country against its enemies, both foreign and domestic.

It is an inalienable right of every man to defend his community, and according to the Constitution, any power not specifically given to the Federal government is the province of the various states, unless it is specifically stated as the right of the citizens in the country. The right to keep and bear arms is a right that is specifically given to the citizens.

The typical liberal's view of this issue is that we need to increase the number of restrictions on the possession of firearms or ban them outright. The conservatives laugh at that notion, stating the obvious fact that criminals do not obey laws so only criminals would be armed.

The average conservative is all about retaining the right to be armed, but most of them do not seem to be disturbed at the idea of registration restriction that would stop some citizens from buying a gun. They do not have a problem with the idea that it is just as unconstitutional to restrict the right to arms as it is to ban them outright.

The way the amendment is written, it is impossible to follow it and still maintain relative safety to the community. Somebody has to find a way to rephrase the Second Amendment such that normal firearms are okay, including the 'assault weapons' that back in my original home state we called 'deer rifles.'

Obviously, the ownership of bombs, nukes, biological weapons, nerve gasses, and other terror weapons will have to be restricted constitutionally if we want to maintain both constitutionality and common sense. It would be nice if the laws we have to obey obeyed in turn the constitutional parameters set forth.

The biggest issue with the changing of the rights of the amendment is that the ordinary citizen has no possibility of arming themselves well enough to stand a chance of putting down a tyrannical government, which was the primary reason that the amendment was created in the first place. I do not see a simple solution to the problem of an insufficiently armed citizenry other than going to extreme lengths to make the Federal government so small that it cannot become a true tyranny.

Whatever we decide will require some pretty intensive discussions about what we **must do** and how much we must abrogate our rights to get it done. This will require a lot of people talking rationally and without any political agendas to fix the problem. I despair of ever seeing such a problem-fixing conference take place.

OCCAM'S RAZOR

THE SUBJECT OF KEEPING and bearing arms in the United States is a particularly thorny one. The fact is that the world that the Constitution was written in no longer exists, and so some of the functions and rights of the Constitution are either impossible or dangerous to maintain in their pure form.

Don't get me wrong. I'm not trying to say that we should abandon the Constitution. On the contrary, I believe we should adhere strictly to it, and when it is very necessary, we will have to change some parts of it to reflect the modern world without giving away the value of the Constitution itself.

The only way that this constitutional republic or any other can survive is if the government that it professes to hold in check remains relatively small. The situations in which the Constitution is outlining the rights and powers of individuals and agencies must also be in keeping with reality.

So let us go back to our argument from the previous chapter. When the Second Amendment was created, there was no distinct difference between civilian arms and military arms; therefore, the Second Amendment made no distinction between the two.

Obviously, in a world of bioweapons, nuclear weapons, intercontinental ballistic missiles, and even more exotic weapons, it is hard to imagine a situation in which we could trust all of humanity with the possession of these various weapons of mass destruction. We know that we certainly cannot trust our or any other government with those same weapons.

We have a central Army that's maintained by the federal government. Any situation where the Second Amendment fulfills its function of protecting the citizens from a tyrannical government would require that we somehow find a way to subtract this overly massive power from the federal government and break it down into segments that would never become part of a tyrannical regime.

Even our current policing agencies and I include in these the FBI, the US marshals, and the various spying agencies such as the CIA and the NSA would be an overpowering force against common citizens in the event that they become part of a tyranny. As I've stated before, our government definitely needs to go on a diet.

The spirit of the Constitution should always be maintained. Without it, we have nothing special in terms of government. With it, we have a remarkable miracle in the form of a kind and caring government.

Occam's razor says that the general solution to our problem is relatively simple. Reduce the size of the federal government. Make sure that the concentration of power never becomes overwhelming in any one set of hands. Make only those changes to the Constitution that reflects the necessities and realities of our new world, and make sure that our judicial branch succeeds in its most important role of evaluating the constitutionality of laws, actions, and situations in general.

The problem with that is the same as finding the solution to any problem. A general solution is a simple matter. We know what in general we have to do. The problem is how we sort through the tangles and issues that arise when we attempt to solve the problem.

In order to solve this problem, we will have to use the services of more constitutional lawyers than currently exist at this time, and we will have to use "just the facts ma'am" type of reasoning, leaving our prejudices and preferences in the other pants at home, if we expect to solve this problem. Of course, we could just do nothing, and wait the short time it's going to take for China to figure out how to take us out the picture.

Personally, I would like for us to solve this problem. I like the Chinese people, but I don't think I'm very good at learning new languages, including Mandarin or Cantonese. So if it's all the same to you, let's just find a way to get this problem solved.

10 BORDERS

A NATION IS DEFINED by the borders it controls, and the people that compose the national citizenry. Both of these parameters are integral to border security.

Our nation currently has no effective border. Our laws and our deployed resources make it impossible to reject any persons that appear at the border and requests entry. Unlike every other functioning nation on this planet, we have laws that diminish our nation's authority to turn back unwanted illegal entries. Of course, this number could never be zero, even assuming that the illegal aliens seeking entry are determined as either a valid or invalid entry.

The matter of illegal immigration has become a political football, which the inferior side obstructing any progress toward a sane process in order to make the superior side look bad. The Republicans claim that the Democrats are hoping to get new voters from the mass of illegals. The Democrats are saying that the Republicans are acting in a racist manner toward the few illegals that make it into our country, and that there is no crisis anyway.

Twenty years ago, the term 'illegal aliens' was commonly used to denote those persons coming across our borders without permission. That has morphed into 'undocumented immigrants,' which has a much more legal connotation.

The term immigrant is defined as persons who move from one locale to another, and it has always carried the implication that that movement was a legal one, breaking no laws in the process. Once the term alien was replaced with the term immigrant, the unconscious supposition is that that person was in the country legally.

Once you substitute the term undocumented for the term illegal, you have now changed the term for persons crossing our border without proper authorization into persons who legally immigrated into the United States without documentation or who have perhaps simply misplaced said documents.

This, of course, is a lie in order to change an illegal activity into a legal one. It is like saying that I went to the bank and made a legitimate withdrawal, without mentioning that I used a gun to convince the bank clerks to give me the money.

When a person comes into our country illegally, he doesn't have a social security number, the right to work in this country, or any of the rights to social services that our citizens have paid for. How is it then that one can come into the country illegally, yet live in the country for years without breaking any laws?

When one enters the country illegally, it is a misdemeanor. When an illegal entry gets a job, the employer is committing a crime. Since you cannot get a paycheck without a social security number, someone has to steal a number from some real citizen, in order to 'legally' work.

In order to use that social security number to live, you would have to file your taxes using it, and it is attached to multiple important documents. Since there is a real citizen also using the number, when the law catches on that there is a crime being committed, they will probably put the innocent citizen through the legal ringer.

If you do use the number to file taxes, then you are committing tax fraud, and probably using a false address, unless you really want to go to jail. If you don't file taxes, then you are guilty of tax avoidance, even if you legitimately paid in the allotted amount of tax withholding.

You must file taxes in order to comply with tax laws. Even though the government is playing with your withholding money, you haven't actually paid your taxes until the tax form is filed. Do you see the paradox?

Once a person enters the country illegally, there is no way that they can remain here without committing multiple crimes in order to do so. In order to remain, they **have to** use the resources that belong to someone else. In order to remain, they have to cause damage to someone else.

Another problem with the illegal alien is a question of fairness. One way or another, each person who steps into the country illegally is also stepping in front of the many people who are trying to enter the country legally.

There is a limit to the resources and activity that can be devoted to maintaining an immigration system. If the resources that go into integrating and ensuring the welfare of the immigrants into our society is used to facilitate the illegal alien's placement, then it is not available for the legal immigrant.

I could write a whole book focusing only on the many facets of border problems and immigrant issues. Since that is not what this book is focused on, let's cut this short, and move on to other subjects that are equally important. Maybe you will be the Author of the Border Book, and I can read all about it.

OCCAM'S RAZOR

No country is sovereign without borders. Any population which can invade your country will, by that act, own your country. Occupation of your country by an outside population makes your country a vassal state of the country from which they come.

Occam's razor suggests that the United States needs a border wall in order to maintain its sovereignty. It truly is the least expensive way to maintain control over illegal immigration across the border.

In addition to a border wall, there is a strong need for legislation to curtail illegal migration over our border. For instance, we need legislation that ends chain migration. Chain migration is where a person arrives legally or illegally, and then one by one, his relatives come into the states to join him.

There also exists a lottery system, where random people who wish to come into the country have their names drawn out of a lottery, which will allow a certain percentage of them to legally immigrate into the country, with no other qualifiers needed.

Instead, Occam's razor suggests that what we need is a merit-based system, similar to those used by many other successful countries to control who among the many becomes eventual citizens of the country. After all, why would we want unskilled immigrants as future citizens, when we can get immigrants with skills and education that we need to take our industry into the next century?

One of the big no-nos about our current immigration system is that it allows people to illegally cross our border and profit by it. If I'd had the fortune to go to preschool, I would've learned that if you do bad things, you don't get rewarded. In order to cross the border illegally, you have to break immigration laws. Why should we reward this behavior when we have so many other deserving applicants?

A few decades ago, I was working in a research lab when a change of ownership caused the company to lay off its entire research wing because they decided they had come to a suitable product. That Friday evening, I was a little distressed to see a beautiful female Chinese engineer sobbing in the parking lot, because without that job, she would wind up having to go back to China.

That Chinese engineer was trying her best to do it all the right way. I do not believe that any person who breaks the laws, and therefore metaphorically butts in line, should profit from their larceny. The people who bothered to learn our language, and do the painstaking paperwork that is necessary to become a citizen should always be at the front of the line for becoming citizens.

If you go to Mexico, and you wish to retire there, you will find that you cannot buy a house as an American citizen. Only Mexican nationals can own property in Mexico. You can either get a Mexican corporation to own the house, or you can essentially lease the house for your lifetime.

If we had such a law ourselves, not only would this solve a lot of problems with foreign ownership of limited American resources, but it would probably also go a long ways toward limiting the damage that China can do in our university system and businesses as China attempts to raid our country for intellectual and financial properties and advantages.

One could actually go on for just about forever on the subject of border control and immigration laws. Which way you go on your opinion depends on relatively small differences in values.

For instance, there are many people who consider the border to be unnecessary and a hindrance to some sort of global agenda. In my opinion, they run afoul of the political equivalent to the socialist financial corundum.

For the most part, the people who consider a border fence to be a waste of time, and who oppose the modification of our immigration laws to a more restrictive form are guilty of a form of thought that where I come from would be thought to originate from a brain located in a pointy head. The argument is this. If we control our borders and immigration into our country, then we potentially maintain our status as a country. If we do not control our borders and immigration, by definition, we are no longer a country.

We can talk about this subject forever. I think that beyond this point in a book that is not strictly limited to border issues, we would be wasting our time to continue the conversation. Maybe in the next book, but for now, let's get on with new subjects in the upcoming chapters.

11 SOCIAL PROGRAMS

THERE ARE A NUMBER of social programs, both current and proposed that exist in that dubious zone between utility and constitutionality. Some of them are considered to be giveaways to the needy, while others are programs made and paid for by the users themselves, such as social security.

With the horde of social programs that exist, or are proposed, it is difficult to know where to start. When in doubt, let us start with the granddaddy of them all. In case you are wondering, I mean social security itself.

Social security was founded back in a time before my birth to make sure the elderly didn't die of starvation. It was supposed to be a self-paying system, where money was paid in by the workers, and then it was distributed to them when they retired.

There is something pretty hinky about how it works. Besides the problem of having a large population of seniors that live longer and a smaller population of current workers, there is also the problem of where does the money go?

When you pay in the money, the Federal Reserve issues a new United States bond to be the 'earning' form of the money. It is that bond that remains as part of the reserve, while the money that you paid in is, to be blunt, not accounted for.

When it comes time for the money to be paid out to you upon retirement, the Federal Reserve creates all-new digital currency out of thin air to pay you off. Since the Fed replaces your money with an imaginary bond when you pay it in, and pays you with imaginary money when you retire, there is a lot of money that is unaccounted for. Can you say 'black projects' and 'pay-offs?'

When social programs are created, both private and governmental, there is a great deal of the money that never gets to where it is supposed to go. Did you know that charities are only required to use five percent of the money they receive to fulfill the actual purpose they exist to serve?

The rest of the money goes to overhead, usually inflated salaries for middle and upper management. The waste of public funds is even more pronounced when the government is in control of the social program.

I am a great believer in the idea that we need systems to ensure that we remain healthy, resource-rich, and happy all the days of our lives, but the government is the worst possible controller of any such program. The fact is that all of these programs consist of the unconstitutional control of our citizenry by the Federal government.

I consider myself to be a conservative Libertarian. I love the idea that anyone can go take college classes and get medical treatment for free. I think that everyone should live their lives without having to worry about being homeless, or starving, or being threatened by any threat on their safety or health.

I would vote for any of these things if you could answer one question. Maybe two questions. The first question is, how do we pay for it? Just a hint that the answer should not be more taxes. The second question is, does the activity meet the requirement to abide by all constitutional limits, and does the act of providing these benefits enrich or empower some individuals or agencies that should not be the recipients of such power or money?

Our country is like our families. We are comparatively rich, but while we can have many things we desire, we cannot have everything we desire. If you buy a new car, chances are that you may have to skip a vacation.

The fact is that our country has been thinking of itself as the benefactor of the rest of the world, and much of our wealth goes out to fix the perceived needs of other countries. The problem with that philosophy is answered with an old story.

There once was a man who had plenty to eat. Every day he used a magic bowl to provide him with one bowl of rice, but it would only do that once a day. One bowl of rice would be enough food of one man for the day.

One day, his neighbor came to him and asked him for food, because he was starving. The man was kind, and he divided his bowl of rice with the neighbor equally, and the neighbor was grateful.

Each day, the neighbor would return to the man's house for a half bowl of rice, and each day, he would not be turned away. After a couple of weeks, the man was losing weight, and he realized that he was starving to death because he was sharing his food.

The neighbor had come to expect to eat 'his' share of the food, and he was enraged when the man finally told him that he could not share any more. The neighbor picked up the fire ax and killed the man. Then he took the magic bowl home with him, where he lived happily and selfishly ever after.

The point of this story is that you should take care of yourself first, and then take care of those close to you. Only after all is well within your own circle do you have enough to share with the rest of the world.

We have thousands of leaks of our funds in our leaky old country. Even the obviously necessary social programs such as social security are soon going to starve to death unless something changes radically.

Until we reorganize the way we use our riches, any social programs we institute are 'pie in the sky' programs, seen from the perspective of even the near future. Socialism claims to be a valid system for pooling the needed resources to make social systems work, but a brief view of history proves that socialism does not work as a functional economic system.

One of the biggest problems with any democratic system is the shortsightedness of the voters or their representatives. The politicians are only interested in doing what will get them re-elected. The voters are only interested in what they can get from the system *this* year.

Meanwhile, tyrannical governments such as those of China or Russia can take the long view. They can fund long term goals such as social programs, space exploration, or technology because they do not care how much their citizens suffer to achieve those goals.

It is sad that the same things that make our system of governance promising in regards to human happiness also limits the resources available to fund needed changes. Maybe someday we will find a way to make it possible to set and get truly long-term goals without making some segment of our population suffer the consequences.

We are not there yet. Until we find a way to make our human natures independently ethical, thoughtful, and find a proper mixture of selfish desires and love of our neighbors, we will not be very good at creating social programs.

We will dissect this and other areas of interest in future chapters. Meanwhile, we have a lot of other aspects of American Politics to cover in the next chapters. It is time to check this subject against Occam's Razor. See you there!

OCCAM'S RAZOR

THE FACT IS THAT WE can do many things to make life easier for our more unfortunate citizens, but we cannot do everything. Our nation is relatively rich, but even the wealth of nations has its limits.

I am a hardcore Libertarian, so I love the idea of free education, free healthcare, and economic security for all of our citizens, but these things are expensive, and someone will have to pay for them.

There are a lot of obstacles to our getting all of these freebies that might be dismantled to make it easier to get the freebies. Education costs so much because it has become easy to get loans to pay for it. Healthcare is expensive because someone invented the idea of health insurance, so the doctor can charge whatever the insurance will pay for, instead of having to bring their fees in line with what the patient can afford.

If the government wasn't there to screw up the management, social programs such as food stamps and welfare could be part of the largesse that the average American commonly contributes to the needy. Social security was originally a savings program for workers to retire on, and if the government wasn't raiding it all of the time, it still could work.

One of the biggest problems with achieving true and beneficial social programs is a strange and irrational belief that everything should be fair. The fact is that life itself is not fair.

When we say "they should pay their fair share" what we are really saying is that there is someone out there who is richer than us, and we believe that they should give us handouts. There are a few people in the world who circumvent the laws and seek to benefit at the expense of others. That phrase about fair share suggests that these are the people we are talking about, but actually it is referring to anyone who owns a business or has substantial wealth, regardless of their personal character.

The two strong foundations of our country are the creation of a just Constitution and the establishment of a strong capitalist system with civilian oversight. These are the tools that we should be looking to when we attempt to better our lives. Any time that we attempt to pacify the masses in the means by which we effect change, we will descend to the lowest common denominator of human nature. If we want to achieve lofty goals, in social or any other areas, we must adhere to lofty ideals.

The subject of social programs is another one of those political arguments that can go on forever. Most of us have been over and over this subject, so there's no real reason to walk down the same well-beaten path. I think it may be time to open up a new topic. Check out the next chapter!

12 MEDICAL

I AM GETTING SOMEWHAT long in the tooth (translate that as old), so I am not immune to struggling mightily with the cost of medical attention. As you might guess, writing is satisfying but not a field where you easily get wealthy.

Americans are currently caught in a trap when it comes to medicine. Even medical insurance supplied through your employer costs far more than it should, and most people struggle to pay for it, and then to pay the copayments.

Forget about Obamacare. It winds up costing you more than employer-supplied insurance in premiums, and then you have thousands of dollars of deductibles to pay out of pocket before the benefits can kick in. You have to be independently wealthy to use the damn thing.

Up until the 1950s, medical insurance did not exist, at least for the general population. Doctors had to provide care within the budget of the patients, meaning for the few bills actually within their wallets at the time of service.

Insurance acts just like a form of credit. Once you start using credit, the vendors of merchandise and services no longer have to limit their bills to what you can pay out of pocket. They are only limited by what the insurance will pay for, and this allows the cost of service to skyrocket upwards.

You see the same inflation of costs happening for any merchandise or services for which credit is the source of payment. The cost of vehicles, houses, education, and medical care have all soared to hundreds of percents of the original costs since we started using credit to pay for them.

I would love to never have to worry about the cost of medical treatment again. Most of us would gladly take free treatment, but nothing is free. If we let the government take over supplying medical care, the cost will spiral up out of control.

The fact is that government is not the answer to anything other than the coordination of armed forces and the enforcement of arrangements made between individuals, states, and other countries. It cannot properly manage medicine, education, or social programs in general.

Our legislature has fallen into the habit of thinking that the best way to enact new laws is to make sweeping changes. They think that a comprehensive medical system change is needed when a hundred or so minor changes would do the trick far more easily, and the end result would be much more appropriate.

For some reason, they think that it is necessary to make everyone a part of a system enacted to attend to the few millions who had no current health insurance. How much easier would it have been to leave what worked alone, and just put systems into place that would protect the medically indigenous population?

Everyone knows the old saying, "If it ain't broke, don't fix it." While there is much to be improved about medical care overall, why does the federal government insist on disrupting the parts that work, and delivering a useless system to the whole of the American population?

The mess our medical system is currently in is a symptom of the basic weaknesses of any democratic system, especially if the voters are being represented by representatives with their own agendas.

OCCAM'S RAZOR

Healthcare is definitely one of the more intricate problems that modern man has to solve. The first question is what limits do we set, and how much are we willing to pay. If there are no limits, then this particular thorny problem is intractable.

For instance, currently, there is a strong push by the liberal contingent of our society to provide free medical care for all of the illegal immigrants that arrive at our hospitals. They fail to mention that many if not most Americans have inadequate healthcare available themselves.

In order to figure out a proper solution to medical issues, we probably need to look at our past in the field of healthcare. Back in the day, the physician would frequently make house calls, diagnose, treat, and receive payment at the home. The payment was usually feasible payments for that farmer or tradesmen to make, although it never was easy to make.

It was not until a variation a credit commonly called insurance came along that doctors found that they could charge extravagant amounts for their treatment of the patient. Their argument for the practice was that it costs a great deal of money to ensure that their diagnosis and treatment were proper. There were always willing attorneys to sue for malpractice if a treatment ever turned out badly.

In order to bring costs within reason, we would need tort reform, practice for cash format, and the willingness of the patients and the doctors to accept that the doctors are human and can always be wrong. Most of the very expensive tests that the doctors currently foist upon the patients are purely to prevent malpractice suits from being created.

Beyond that, we need to set the limits on what a person can expect from the medical industry in protecting them from disease. In the near future, none of this may actually matter, because I foresee a time when medical treatment will be entirely instrumental. The use of nanotech and related technology will ensure our health beyond any expectations we could currently have.

So there it is. If we can just make it through a few more years, then we will probably see a medical world that is a paradise in comparison to the current one. All we have to do is to live to see that day.

That will be enough nattering about medicine for now. I am sure that we will be circling back to it in a future chapter.

13 FASCIST ENCROACHMENT

———— ❦ ————

I WAS WATCHING FOX news today, and I saw the face of fascism. It was an earnest-seeming conversation between a Republican opinion journalist and a Democratic Talking Head.

Fascism is an attitude of a group regarding power. Let us take a quick look at Hitler, who is the world's best known Fascist.

Hitler was well known for his oratory. He convinced a nation that they had a destiny which required the subjugation or execution of all other races except for the 'Aryans,' and formed groups such as the Brownshirts and the SS to complete the tasks necessary to reach that insane goal.

Fascism is not a particular form of government in and of itself. Nations, companies, or any other group of people, can be Fascists. Fascism is an attitude toward what is necessary and acceptable in obtaining the power to do what the group wants to be done, and it is based on a belief that the Fascist is superior to opposing groups.

The typical tool used by Fascists is an emotional argument. They convince others that they believe are worthy that their beliefs are Truth. They also convince their new majority that they should not tolerate any non-believers or those of inferior worth.

One can generally recognize a Fascist argument by two of the most common features. The first feature is that they have a deficit of facts that support their argument, but they make an art form out of avoiding situations where they are confronted and forced to admit the fallacy of their argument. The second feature is that they will "talk over" their opponents, never giving them a chance to argue their points, or to point out the absurdity of the Fascist position.

When I was listening to that FOX broadcast, I noted both of these features in the arguments put forward by the Democratic Talking head. He adroitly avoided any mention of the many facts that are obvious that made his argument stupid, and he would immediately continue talking when the show host would begin to question his logic at a noise level high enough to ensure that nobody could make sense of what the host was saying.

Don't get me wrong. The host did two things wrong. He did not point out the fallacies in the Fascist argument when he was confronted with them, and he did not turn off the microphone of the Democrat when he began his talk-over process.

I can hear you telling me that the talking head could not be a Fascist since he was a Democrat, which is now code for a democratic socialist. That brings us back to our first point.

Stalin imposed socialism on the Russian people, but he did it by Fascist methods. Just like Hitler, he gave the people a belief to believe in, and then he used that belief to impose his will on the people.

He gave the people the belief that the people could control their own country, sharing everything more or less evenly, and deciding what they wanted in a vaguely defined democratic process. Once they believed that ideal, he used them to seize power and installed himself as the holder of that power.

In the Soviet Union, they have elections, but somehow, the elections always re-elect the persons that are already in power, no matter how decrepit the world around them is becoming. Work becomes slavery, plenty becomes low-grade starvation for the bulk of the citizens, and the persons in power accumulate opulent wealth without providing any reasonable service to earn it.

One of the more insidious signs that Fascism is at work is the use of already existing structures, agencies, and groups to pursue the goals of the Fascist sector. This we see taking place in our country right now.

During the Obama days, I was alarmed to hear about a website that urged American citizens to watch their neighbors and turn them in for any vague possibility of a crime that the tattletale could conceive of happening. During those years, the Obama administration also used the IRS to harass various conservative groups.

Several agencies were used to run false flag operations on the American people. The Fast and Furious scandal was allegedly a sting on the Mexican cartels, but it was actually a way to hyperinflate the number of weapons in the hands of violent criminals, and thereby justify antigun legislation.

One of the biggest Fascist moves in this country that has ever happened was the so-called "Patriot Act," which basically suspends all American's rights to privacy and all other civil and constitutional rights. As long as that sucker sticks around, the government can basically enslave any citizen at a moment's notice.

Our country is well along the path toward Fascism. Our Penal system is the biggest one in the world. Most of our constitutional rights have been compromised or subverted. The technical tools that exist are far beyond anything envisioned by the Founding Fathers, and the government can pry into any of our affairs legally without any limits.

We lost our freedom to legislative manipulations sometime early in the 1900s. If we do not do some intelligent repairs, we will go down in history as a nation of slaves.

OCCAM'S RAZOR

THE PRINCIPAL CAUSE of a Fascist regime is ignorance on the part of the citizenry. Fascism cannot endure unless people except propaganda as the truth. In order to prevent the slow creep of fascism into government, one has to be intellectually involved with the political situation, and they have to operate from a position of honorable intentions.

All governments receive their power from the population. Regardless of how many factions there are that attempt to take power by force of arms, it cannot happen unless the population accepts it. Most of the time, the population does accept it because it does not want to suffer the pain that not accepting it brings to them.

To avoid fascism forever, the average citizen has to be intelligent, honorable, generous, and one hell of a stoic. The moment you accept something to avoid pain, the person who brings you pain wins, and you lose.

In order to bring yourself to a state of Stoicism, you have to reach that moral level where doing the wrong thing is never acceptable and doing the right thing is always the correct way to go for you. I sometimes despair of seeing common humanity become this ethical, but they really have no choice if they want to avoid a degeneration of government, and the attendant chaos that that degeneration causes.

That is enough of this particular subject for now. We will wrap all this up in a cute little bow at the end of the book. For now, it is time to get on to other subjects.

14 COMMUNISM

COMMUNISM IS A STRANGE branch of socialism which says that the population actually owns all the resources of that government. Of course, where the problem comes in, is that there are always disconnected rulers who administrate that resource bounty.

One of the problems with the concept of communism is it doesn't work. You probably have experienced this yourself in your family life. If you have a family where some of the people don't work, and part of the family supports them all, then you probably have at least one or two of the members who don't even try to contribute to the family's well-being.

Communism has this problem precisely. It also has a problem of governing bodies or persons who have an excellent opportunity to skim the wealth of the nation before reluctantly dispensing a small amount of that wealth to the population. It is probably a proper time for me to point to Venezuela in regards to this particular phenomena.

Russia is a prime example of the natural consequence of beginning to go down the communist role Road. The dispensers of the wealth began to keep most of it for themselves. When this became a standard, the dispensers became oligarchs, and the common workers became no more than slaves.

Communism is a fine ideal, but in order for it to work; one must find a way to eliminate the middleman. It may not work well with an absolute democracy, provided part of the democratic process was to make all of the day-to-day decisions collectively. This is unlikely to ever be feasible because people aren't that interested in taking care of things themselves, and because people are not interested in taking on more responsibility.

OCCAM'S RAZOR

This section will be a simple one because the concept of communism goes against the feral nature of man. Unless mankind becomes a species of adults, communism can never work. Therefore, we can sum up the solution in the one simple following sentence.

DON'T DO IT.

15 MoNEY

THE MONEY THAT A COUNTRY uses defines that country in a more intimate way than almost any other factor you could name. At its simplest, money is a medium of exchange that reflects the value of work and resources available for sale.

In the deep past, most people traded with each other using a barter system. In barter, one would trade something they had of value to someone who didn't have that thing for something of value the other one had that the first person wanted.

It used to be that the things traded consisted of materials, food, or perhaps work. One of the items that people always liked was gold. Over time, people begin minting gold coins with known values as a medium of exchange.

Things went on this way for several centuries. Eventually, someone had the bright idea to simply create paper promissory notes with a specific value payable to the holder of the note. This eventually evolved into our modern currency.

Every country in the world produces its own currency at this point. Some of the currencies, such as the currency of Zimbabwe, are not worth the paper that they are printed on. The currency of the United States has always been considered to be of premium value because we out-produce the rest of the world, and this was reflected in the strength of our dollar.

Things have evolved even more. Decades ago, a cartel of independent bankers got together and managed to con the government into accepting them as the caretakers of our currency. They created the Federal Reserve, which is a nongovernmental agency that prints our money and controls our interest rates.

One of the problems with the Federal Reserve is that they do not see a problem with creating money out of thin air, and they certainly enjoy setting up systems which enrich them, using the imaginary money that they create to buy real products and services. Until earlier this century (or should I say last century) our currency was pegged to the gold value, even though trading it for gold was severely restricted.

Now, of course, our currency is not really pegged to anything, unless you take into account the petroleum trade, which somebody has managed to con the world into believing they must use our dollars to trade for oil. This, of course, is a problem, because sooner or later the rest the world will realize that the dollar does not have an intrinsic value.

Returning to the gold standard is not a realistic solution. There is not enough gold in the world to back our currency, and if there was, the gold standard would collapse as soon as people realized that they could not actually trade the dollars for gold.

It is possible of course to make a new standard based on actual resources, which would consist of work, products, or resources, but it would be a nightmare to keep tabs on the real values of all of these items and to rein in the number of dollars in existence to correlate with resources available.

Additionally, there is the problem of the intangibles. For instance, how does one value intellectual properties, such as artistic or business ideas, and where exactly do they fit into the total value allotted for the system?

There is a very thorny problem with trying to control currency. There is always someone in charge, which will attempt to gain power or wealth from the process. There is always some resource or data that is important to controlling that currency that will not be accounted for.

It was not until this decade that we truly possessed the computational power to possibly control the currency values. We now have computers that are smart enough to keep tabs on all this for us, if we can only figure out how to keep them secure from outside interference.

OCCAM'S RAZOR

Occam's razor would suggest that the solution to our money problems is simple in theory. Peg the dollar to the available resources, and assign a dedicated computer system to keep tabs on the balance.

Dismiss the Federal Reserve. They have no positive value to us, and they are a distinct risk. Since interest rates are a function of currency surpluses or deficits, or they are assigned in consideration of investment risk, the control of interest rates which a Federal Reserve currently does can be done as well or probably much better by the computer system.

Money is another one of those subjects which one could write a whole book about. I'm not really interested in doing that, so let's move on from this subject. On to the next chapter!

16 CURRENT INSANITY

OUR CURRENT POLITICAL scene is a mess. If a person is a problem solver, he usually likes to attack one problem at a time. We don't have one problem with our political scene. We have a large number of problems to solve.

There has been a large invasion of our political rhetoric by people who use typical socialist tactics in order to attempt to win their political wars. This starts by using flawed but unassailable arguments in defense of their positions and using any means necessary to sway the population to their point of view.

There are a number of billionaires who own the leading news sources and are solidly on the side of these socialists and their agendas. This has given them the power to turn most of our news outlets into propaganda machines.

Nontraditional news outlets, such as Facebook and Google, contribute to this propaganda war in a big way. They are on the side of the "liberals," and they have done an extensive job of promoting the liberal point of view while suppressing the conservative point of view. The big four newscasts on the airwaves including CNN, ABC, CBS, and NBC have wholeheartedly given themselves over to the liberal viewpoint.

More than simply promoting the liberal agenda, these entities have made every effort to demonize the conservative and even the libertarian viewpoints. It has come to the point where the general population will soon come to conflict of a more physical nature if something is not done soon to correct this tendency to propagandize the news.

Among the many destructive tendencies of the liberal media and policies is the idea of opposing any enforcement of border control, single-minded opposition to all policies of the current president, and a straightforward desire to reinvent our history in a way which is beneficial to the liberal agenda and destructive to the conservative agenda. You may have noticed this effort in the widespread attempt to censor or dismantle all monuments that have any element expressed which does not conform to the liberal viewpoint.

This has been ongoing for three or four decades now in our educational system. The curriculum that is currently being taught conforms in large part to the liberal agenda. The obvious view here is that if you teach the young false but useful facts, they will continue to believe them throughout their lives. This has in large part shown itself to be true, as more and more of the younger generations have expressed socialist or sometimes even anarchist viewpoints.

The obvious problem, of course, is that when the number of young voters with socialist leanings becomes the majority, we will be a socialist state. Soros and other wealthy social engineers are aware of this, and they have spent hundreds of millions of dollars to ensure that this disastrous world of the globalist comes about.

Unfortunately, even the conservative have these globalist elites embedded in their politics. The Koch brothers also have a globalist agenda, even though it is of a more libertarian viewpoint. They have no particular interest in protecting the country's borders, or in maintaining the country as a discrete and sovereign nation.

Yes, the national politics are definitely in a mess. The conservative viewpoint still has a slight majority, but more and more of the younger voters have been conditioned into believing that realistic and rational positions are not necessary to solve our problems.

Conservatives can be attacked for the simple act of going to a conservative rally, or even for wearing a MAGA hat. Groups such as ANTIFA have proliferated throughout the country, and now pose a significant risk for anyone choosing to use their freedom of speech if their viewpoint is that of a conservative.

One of the problems that have come well into the light is the idea of freedom of speech on college campuses. It has come to the point where conservative speakers and even students that are seen by the liberal masses to have conservative viewpoints are no longer welcome. Without the opportunity for the students to hear all sides of any argument, the student body will never learn any ideas except those force-fed to them by the Globalists.

There seem to be two major agendas in motion, attempting to determine the future of the world. The first is a nationalist agenda, which seeks to define and protect nations as separate entities of the world. The second agenda is a global agenda, which seeks to combine all of the planet under the umbrella of one major power structure.

These two agendas are not monolithic. For instance, the nationalist agenda that currently prevails in the United States is obviously not the same as that of China, and the two sub-agendas are at odds with each other.

The European Union can be pointed to as an example of the globalist agenda. It is not the only example of that genre of agenda, however. The Chinese system may aspire to become a globalist one, only with the Chinese at the epicenter. Even the Arabic world might be seen as a religion based globalist idea.

Any system that seeks to create an empire, assimilating other countries into the system, is, in essence, a globalist system if it seeks to assimilate those other countries as more than a mere expansion of real estate. America is not such a system since we have the strange habit of invading and defeating, then rebuilding the countries we invade, before giving them back to the inhabitants.

The true essence of the problem confronting us is which of these two philosophies, Nationalism or Globalism, will win the war of the human future. Each of them has traits worth having, but each of them is antithetical to the other.

Each of these agendas also has its weaknesses. Nationalism protects the specific cultures, citizens, and possessions of the nation, but to some extent, it also is naturally isolating. It does not necessarily provide the nation with a global backup in the case of need, whereas, the globalist agenda subsumes all of the neighbors of any part of the culture that is threatened. These other parts of the culture can be coerced into protecting the entire organism.

The globalist agenda does not value ethnic or cultural diversity, and it will, over time, eliminate all of these differences in its population. While this is not necessarily a detriment to its survival, it may turn out to be proof that the security it provides to the human species might be found to be valueless. What is the value of saving the human body, when you take away everything that makes the person human?

We have giant problems to solve in our future. We will need to become a space-faring species if we wish for the human species to survive for long. We need to become much more adroit at learning and using that knowledge to survive ecological and human-caused disasters in the near future.

It is likely that one day soon, we will meld some aspects of Nationalism and Globalism to make a superior form of system that will serve our needs in the future. It will be necessary to preserve cultural differences. It will also be necessary to be able to cooperate on a much grander scale than we currently can.

I could be cynical here and suggest that this is too steep of a hill for us to climb, but what real choice do we have? Either we will learn how to form a system of government more like a sensible version of the Star Trek Federation, or we will ultimately fall before the inevitable barbarians. It is our choice.

The last section of this book will attempt to suggest some of the possible steps we could take to climb out of this hole that we have dug for ourselves. We will reference Occam's Razor as we suggest these baby steps. See you there!

OCCAM'S RAZOR

THIS WILL BE THE FINAL chapter in this book, and it needs to wrap the problems of American Politics up in a neat little package and suggest some solutions to the problems we face. If we can't see our way to the solutions, we should at least attempt to point in the proper direction. It is a big task, and I am not sure that I or anyone can do it justice, but I will give it a try.

I will attempt to break the problem down into two parts. The first part will deal with addressing the fundamental causes of the issues that are becoming problems. The second part will deal with the mechanics or strategies of dealing with more specific problems.

The primary problem we have in this country is with the distribution of power. The Executive Branch has become greatly bloated due to attempting to deal with the powers ceded to it by an inept Congress. The Congress has become nearly useless, as each faction spends most of its time fighting with all the other factions. Politics has infected the Judiciary and become more important to many of its judges than the Constitution.

We need to constrain or limit the powers of the various branches of government to their assigned constitutional powers. If we do this, we will limit the size of government to a form that is drastically smaller than the size it is currently, which will not be easy.

The Executive Branch is the one that is easiest to see how excessive the growth beyond the original intentions has been. There was never a power over education, environment, housing, or any other such areas intended, and exercising power over them is both unconstitutional and a very bad idea. Most of these areas are the province of state powers, and that never should have been abrogated to the Federal Government.

The first item on the To-Do list should be the abolishment of such agencies as HUD, the Department of Education, and the hundreds of similar agencies. They are not needed or practical, and we should get rid of them.

Along with abolishing these agencies, there are thousands of laws, regulations, and policies dealing with those areas that should be repealed. Once the agencies and their attendant laws have been abolished, if there are any disputes between the states or individuals dealing with the subject matter, that is what the court system exists to clarify.

If, for example, Arizona is contaminating the waters of the Colorado River before it flows into California, then the proper form of relief is for the State of California to take the State of Arizona to court. This has always been the real method for dealing with such disputes. The Federal Agencies simply added an additional unneeded layer to the problem.

I have always been a bit confused about what state got the waters of the Colorado first, so forgive me if I mangled the plaintiff and defendant positions there. The simple fact is that the courts are the correct arena to dispute transgressions of this sort, and the resources of the states belong to the states to argue about, not the Feds.

Once we have reduced the size of government, we also need to do something about the amount of power that individuals in government have amassed. This means that we need to have term limits for every government official, and we need to eliminate all lobbying except for the support of specific matters that are specific and local to the representative's territory of representation. This means *no more paid lobbyists*. Period.

Politics has always acted like a popularity contest. Back in the old days, everyone knew the prospective politician, and they voted for him because they liked him, and knew that he would vote for or against the things that meant something to them. Now that the voting populations are bigger, they no longer are sure for what he would vote. They like him for the same reason that many first dates end in disaster. After all, just because he has a pretty face doesn't mean that he is a good man.

It would probably be a good idea for any person who runs for office first to have to pass some sort of test of the same sort that employers use to gauge whether a prospective employee has the skills for the job. There are many forms that the test could take, but it would be useful to be sure that the fellow is competent. There are a lot of pretty idiots out there.

The second part of this first part deals with the kind of modifications we need to make to our laws to make things work out. I will give you two examples.

As I write this, there has been an incident where ANTIFA in masks beats up a conservative journalist. There is a current debate on if we should or should not allow them to wear masks while they are protesting. People are suggesting that it is a matter of first amendment rights.

If I am not mistaken, cops will meet you if you wear a mask into a bank to withdraw money. They will also arrest you if you yell "FIRE" in a crowded theatre. Free speech should never require a mask. It should be considered the same as intending to commit a crime in these sorts of circumstances and made a criminal act in itself.

The second example is the Patriot Act. Besides such wonderful features of that act as being able to declare martial law at discretion, it also allows a virtually unlimited ability to spy on anyone for anything.

Although the more liberal of my readers will doubt it, it was used extensively on the Trump campaign to attempt a soft coup on his administration. As he says, it should never be allowed to happen to another president. or to anyone else.

That should be a good sampling of the sort of things that need to be done to get our country started back down the right path. Now, let us talk about the more fundamental stuff.

There is no doubt about it. We need some solid reforms of the Constitution to work more solidly with the modern world. Judicial precedent is supposed to keep the laws working with current conditions, but there is just so much they can do. Time for a lot of people to get together and make some changes that are still very much in keeping with the original spirit of the document.

Immigration should be somewhat hard. Citizenship should be a whole lot harder. Immigration laws should make it impossible to enter illegally, and the country should always gain a benefit from the people who come in legally.

The original purpose of the Second Amendment is impossible to fulfill at this point. We cannot allow our population to be armed well enough to stave off a large tyrannical government, but our right to be armed should be potent enough to at least make it hard to put us down like dogs.

Many if not most of the legislation voted into law by the Congress is not constitutional. Such laws do not get challenged until someone can gain standing to take it to court, based on the possible harm that law has caused them.

Many of those unconstitutional laws never are challenged, because in many cases, standing is hard to get. Just endangering a right or freedom is insufficient if no actual infringement of that right or freedom can be shown.

Each new piece of legislation should be critiqued by the Judicial Branch in the process of passing it so that our legal system is no longer filled with unconstitutional laws. This could easily be added to the legislative process, somewhere before the president signs it into law.

All of this would require a constitutional convention to modify the document to reflect needed changes. Two considerations *must* be part of that process.

There must be a robust protection of all citizen's rights and freedoms, with a careful allocation of the rights and powers of the Federal and State governments. These considerations must be safeguarded, or the whole idea of improving the function of the governmental organism is doomed to failure.

Immigration laws should be clear and simple. Third country sanctuary is not permitted. No illegal immigrant (alien) is never to be allowed to remain in the country. Current reasons to allow migration should be changed to a merit-based system. Non-citizens should not be allowed to hold a driver's license or vote. They should not work in this country unless they hold a work visa.

Non-citizens should not be allowed to own real property in this country. Instead, they can rent or lease it like in most other countries. This would apply to houses, buildings, and businesses.

We could go on forever with all of these subject areas, but I suspect that you probably need to get some sleep, so I will wrap up this book. I hope that you enjoyed it, and maybe even found something new on which to ponder. Until the next book, enjoy life.

The End

ABOUT THE AUTHOR

JD LOVIL writes both nonfiction and fiction books. He is the writer of several How-To and speculative nonfiction books, as well as several cross-genre science fiction novels, dealing with the existence of a multitude of parallel earths as required by the Many Worlds interpretation of Quantum Theory. Originally from Arkansas, JD Lovil now lives in Phoenix, Arizona.

IF YOU ENJOYED THIS book, please consider leaving an honest and positive review at the site where you purchased it.

You may connect with the Author on Facebook at:

www.facebook.com/jd.lovil.9[1]

You may also connect with the Author on Pinterest:

www.pinterest.com/jdlovil9

You may also connect with the Author by email at

jdlovilpublishing@gmail.com

---

1. https://www.facebook.com/jd.lovil.9

If you enjoyed the book you just read, you might also enjoy
<u>THE LAYMAN'S GUIDE TO QUANTUM REALITY</u>
Here is an excerpt of that book for you:
Chapter Three of
The Layman's Guide to Quantum Reality

3 laws of quantum theory

THE WAY I SEE IT, QUANTUM Theory started as a mathematical exercise in probability calculations, and ended up being an exercise in metaphysics. Quantum equations yield general solutions. A general solution is a 'plug and play' solution. A general solution is a solution, which yields specific solutions when you substitute specific variable values into the general equation. In many cases, one valid solution set of a general solution is the positive and negative number values of 'the answer.'

Because there are more than one specific solutions to quantum equations, it is necessary to calculate a probability of finding the system with which the equation is concerned in one state, versus finding the system in a different state. This simple calculation of probabilities became complicated when Heisenberg came up with his Uncertainty Principle.

Heisenberg stated that certain data must be forbidden to know by the Observer of an event. He was talking about events in the microscopic world of elementary particles, such as electrons. His simple claim that the Observer can know one part of the status of a particle, but knowing that information will exclude the Observer from knowing complimentary information or data about the particle's status at the same time blew a lot of Physicists' minds.

You can know the momentum or location of a particle, but not both at the same time. This was intended to apply to the microscopic level only, and Heisenberg never intended it to apply to the macro-scale universe. Particles are neither particles nor waves but are 'smeared' over the small space most likely to contain them, and this throws some of the variables of calculation into doubt at any particular measurement time.

You can measure the momentum of a particle by observing the effects via the use of your measurement device, or you can detect the particle position using your devices, but measuring either status increases the uncertainty of the other one because the measurement you can make is a probabilistic one rather than a certain and specific one.

Heisenberg was showing that specific solutions could not be made for all aspects of a probability equation because doing so would be to turn a general equation solution of probability into a specific solution with no probability uncertainty. Let us see the form for momentum (p) and velocity (v) of a particle.

The simple equation is

$$\Delta x \Delta p \geq h/4\pi$$

Remember that this equation calculates the uncertainties in x and p in relation to each other:

Δx is the uncertainty in position x

Δp is the uncertainty in momentum p

$h/4\pi$ is a constant number. For our purposes let us call it C and say that it is equal to 1. As a probability calculation, remember that the uncertainty in x or p cannot be zero, nor can the number usefully be incalculable.

$\Delta x \Delta p \geq h/4\pi$ becomes $\Delta x \Delta p \geq C$ becomes $\Delta x \Delta p \geq 1$

$$\Delta x \geq 1/\Delta p \text{ and } \Delta p \geq 1/\Delta x$$

When the uncertainty in position x falls to certainty because it has been measured, by definition and mathematics, the certainty in the momentum p must decrease, and vice versa. We do not have to solve the equation to see that this is true since each of the uncertainties in this equation is in the reciprocal form of each other.

Physicists promptly jumped on the idea of this being a demonstration of 'The Observer Effect.' The Observer effect is the idea that you cannot observe a particle without bumping it with some force used in the measurement, making it different from what the measurement shows after the measurement. While this is generally true in the process, it has nothing to do with Heisenberg's Uncertainty Principle.

A couple of different Observer-related relationships were revealed in the aftermath of deriving the Uncertainty Principle. The first was the effect of observation itself, where the Observer defined the property of the particle by observation and found that he was affecting the uncertainty of the complementary properties by changing the probability mathematics that the observation yielded. The second was the Observer Effect mentioned in the last paragraph, where the act of observation perturbed the system being observed, changing the status of the particle after observation of part of the system of properties.

One of the traditional experiments that demonstrated the effect of an Observer on a quantum system was called the Double Slit Experiment. It has been done in various formats since 1801, and it involved sending a photon or electron toward a plate with two thin slits cut into it, through which the particle can pass, and a photographic plate behind the plate to record which slit the particle came through.

It was noted that the particle would apparently pass through both slits and cause an interference pattern on the photographic plate if nobody was watching the experiment, indicating that it had passed through in its waveform, but it would pass through a single slit as a particle if somebody were watching the experiment. The acuity of observation was important to the results as well. If a high detail camera were placed strategically to watch the experiment, the experiment would show particle properties. Turn the camera off, and the experiment would show wave properties.

A physicist named Schrödinger was irritated by the metaphysical turn that quantum theory was taking, and so he proposed a joke thought experiment that has become known as Schrödinger's cat. This is how it went.

Schrödinger told the tale about a cat, enclosed in a box, with a device that was guaranteed to release poison and kill the cat exactly 50%

of the times that the lid to the box was sealed. The cat had a 50:50 chance of being dead in the box, and the same chance of still being alive.

With tongue in cheek, Schrödinger asserted that the cat was neither alive nor dead until the Observer opened the box and looked inside. At that time, he would see that the cat was alive, or that the cat was dead, and his act of observing that would make it so. He wanted to demonstrate that the metaphysical viewpoint of that situation was ridiculous and that when the Observer opened the box, all that was happening was that he was now able to see which result was the real one. To Schrödinger, it was a simple probability problem, and it had nothing to do with some arcane power that the Observer generated.

The strange thing about Quantum Theory is that Schrödinger was right, and wrong at the same time. The cat in the box was a simple fifty percent probability calculation. The presence or absence of the Observer probably would have had no effect on the outcome of the experiment. Probably.

The double slit experiment indicates that the Observer *is* an integral component of the outcome. In the case of the double slit experiment, the outcome appears to be different when the Observer is present. The Observer resolves which solution is real.

We should note here that quantum events are not usually considered on the Macro level because what we see in our world is a swarm of trillions of particles. Each one of these particles is engaged in quantum activities, but in the quantities that are required for us to notice them, the outcomes of the aggregate events statistically smear out into an aggregate statistical approximation of Standard or Newtonian physics.

We will get deeper into the nature of the Observer's interaction with the reality around him or her in a future chapter. For now, let us paint a stranger picture of the quantum world. Only after we discover the true nature of reality can we explore what effect we might have on that reality.

We have touched on the fact that particles of all sorts have both a wave-like and a particle-like nature. The fact is that everything shares in this wavicle nature, but for macro-objects, the statistical smearing causes the wavicle nature to pass unnoticed.

In what I will call Traditional Quantum Theory, all 'particles' have both a wave and a particle form. Since all of the Macro Objects we see around us are composed of these particles, they too have this 'wavicle' form. The reason we do not see the waveform of the matter around us is due to the statistical nature of large numbers of particles. Just as large numbers of charged objects tend to cancel charges, so too does a large number of waveforms tend to cancel each other.

In Standard Quantum Theory, all transitions of energy levels, and therefore of the position are instantaneous and nonlocal. There are minimums of distance and duration which are indivisible. This is because everything, including space and time, is quantized. No duration of time exists less than

$$10^{-43} \text{ s}$$

There is no distance or length that exists that is less than

$$1.6 * 10^{-23} \text{ m}$$

These are the Planck distance and duration constants. Think of time and distance are composed of bricks of these sizes, instead of little points with no volume. Since there is no distance less than $1.6 * 10^{-23}$ m, if a particle is moving, it must of necessity instantaneously jump or teleport at least these tiny distances in the process. Only if space is composed of a substance with no minimum distance can Newtonian movement work without some form of discontinuous 'teleportation.' Otherwise, teleportation must be a part of the movement process.

These events are not restricted to be local events. They have smaller but still valid chances of being nonlocal. These transitions of distance are valid for any distance larger than the Planck minimum. It is not forbidden for an electron to transit to extra-galactic positions, although the chances in any one case are vanishingly small.

Let me give you an example of a nonlocal event. As we know, Einstein claimed that there was no speed greater than the speed of light. If we wish to act or transmit information, you cannot do so at any speed greater than the speed of light. Quantum Theory disputes this by the concept of entangled particles. We will get back to what that means in a moment.

Assume that we are flying across empty space in the good ship Lollipop when some unknown god decides to materialize a star about a light year away. Einstein said that our ship would not feel the gravity from that ship for a year, at the same time that we could see the star existed by the light that had just traveled to us.

Quantum Theory says not so fast. We have changed the information that is part of the quantum equation for the system, and this information may be able to travel at any speed. If an electron can travel galactic distances instantaneously in a small percentage of electron transitions, you may also feel the effect of a new gravitational well a light year away instantaneously.

If it takes a year to feel the effects of the new gravitational source, that is an example of a local process. If it is felt instantaneously, or less than a year later, it is a nonlocal process.

Quantum entanglement is a nonlocal process. If two electrons interact with each other, it has been shown from a series of experiments that the properties that each display may be affected by what is done to the other one, no matter where they are in relation to each other. If you flip the spin on one of the electrons, the spin on the other one may also flip, no matter how far away the second electron is away from the first one.

The subject of nonlocal events and entanglement will come up in many guises in the chapters of this book, but now we return to a primary component of Quantum Theory. Quantum states are calculated for any considered system using the Schrödinger equation. I will not be going through the Schrödinger equation here, as it is a little more complicated than I suspect that most of my Readers want to get in mathematical explanations of the theory.

The solution to the Schrödinger equation is a general solution. This means that the solution of the equation is another equation that will yield the specific solutions that apply if you have specific parameters, or that will yield the set of all specific solutions. For instance, if you have a general solution of

x=n where n is defined as the set of all integers

...-3,-2,-1.0, 1, 2, 3...

Then specific solutions can include x=-3 or x=0 or x=2 and so on.

The point is that quantum equations have more than one solution. Standard quantum theory says that only one of these solutions turns out to be the True solution, and the rest of them are just potential answers that turn out not to be the correct one. Going back to the double slit experiment, this meant that the electron had a 50:50 chance of going through either of the slits in the plate.

The fact that the unobserved experiment indicated that the electron went through **both** slits suggested to the Experimenters that the equation was ***unresolved***. This meant that if the experiment was unobserved, the correct solution was not made real. It was only if somebody observed the experiment that one of the two possibilities showed itself to be real.

In Standard Theory, this meant that the Observer's presence was necessary to resolve which of the solutions was real, and collapse all of the other forms of the equation, making only one of the solutions real. The rest of the solutions were unreal.

Seen one way, this just meant that the Observer was a part of the system necessary to collapse an equation solution set into one true one and other false ones. Seen another way, the Observer occupies a metaphysical position of power in the creation of our reality.

In the great year of my birth, Hugh Everett proposed a theory that came to be known as The Many Worlds Theory. This theory said that all solutions to a quantum equation were true. When the Observer resolved a particular solution as true, he resolved it for just his universe. The decision point of each event was a place that the universe would branch into a new worldline for each of the possible solutions for that event.

This meant that if the Observer saw that the electron went through the left slit of the two slits, that was true for the universe in which the Observer continued to experience. However, the Observer would also see that it had passed through the right slit in another universe, which had split off from the common worldline at the instant of the event.

I am not going into any more detail on the Many World Theory at this point since I will be covering the subject extensively in the next few chapters, and aspects of the theory in several subsequent chapters. Put on your protective helmets. It is going to be a wild ride!

Don't miss out!

Visit the website below and you can sign up to receive emails whenever JD Lovil publishes a new book. There's no charge and no obligation.

https://books2read.com/r/B-A-XMCC-EWAAB

BOOKS 2 READ

Connecting independent readers to independent writers.

Also by JD Lovil